BATHROOM of TEXAS TRIVIA

Weird, Wacky and Wild

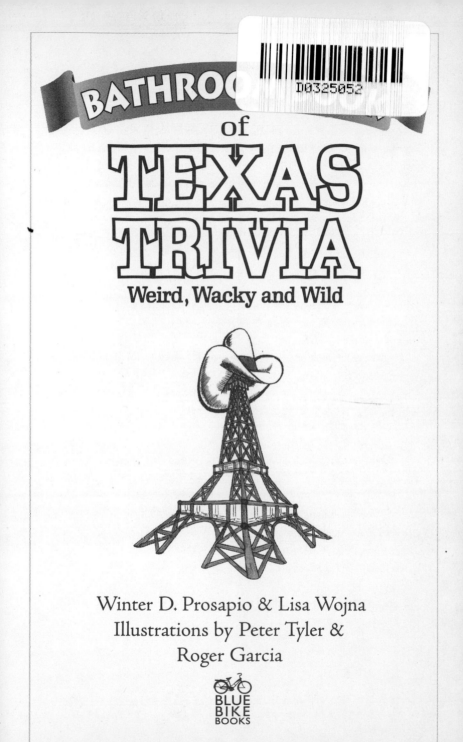

Winter D. Prosapio & Lisa Wojna
Illustrations by Peter Tyler &
Roger Garcia

BLUE
BIKE
BOOKS

The Publisher: Blue Bike Books
www.bluebikebooks.com

Library and Archives Canada Cataloguing in Publication

Prosapio, Winter, 1962–
      Bathroom book of Texas trivia : weird, wacky and wild / Winter D. Prosapio and Lisa Wojna.

ISBN-13: 978-1-897278-30-7
ISBN-10: 1-897278-30-6

      1. Texas—Miscellanea. I. Wojna, Lisa, 1962– II. Title.
F386.6.P76 2007   976.4   C2007-902629-X

Project Director: Nicholle Carrière
Project Editor: Sheila Quinlan
Illustrations: Peter Tyler, Roger Garcia
Cover Image: Roger Garcia

We acknowledge the support of the Alberta Foundation for the Arts for our publishing program.

DEDICATION

To Adam, Sierra and Mireya, who now know more about Texas trivia than they ever wanted to.

−Winter

ACKNOWLEDGMENTS

Thanks to the dozens of people who dropped delicious trivia in my lap and kept sending more. Thanks to my husband and daughters, who have been endlessly encouraging, as well as to my parents and sister. I'm sending out an embrace to my friends, who believed in me well before I did. And one special side note to my big sister (who inexplicably fled the state long ago): I talked to the governor, Christy. You can come back now.

−Winter

Many thanks to my clever editor, Sheila, who pieced together the work of two authors and did so seamlessly; and to my family—my husband Garry, sons Peter, Matthew and Nathan, daughter Melissa and granddaughter Jada. Without you, all this and anything else I do in my life would be meaningless.

−Lisa

CONTENTS

INTRODUCTION

The novelist John Steinbeck said it best: "Texas is a state of mind. Texas is an obsession. Above all, Texas is a nation in every sense of the word."

For 10 short years, Texas was an independent nation. They were bloody years, filled with war and tremendous financial cost. Yet somehow, the founding of the Republic of Texas and its 10 years of existence was an experience so profound that the streak of independence, the palpable sense of identity separate from the rest of the country, is still going strong.

Even today, many natives consider themselves Texans first and Americans second. Texans are notoriously proud of not only their victories, but of their losses and of their heroes and villains.

Consider this: every child in Texas readily recognizes the state flag. Even first graders can sketch it out for anyone who asks. Texas has had a state pledge since 1933, but it was relatively obscure. Starting in 2001, it became law for all school districts to require students to pledge allegiance to the U.S. and Texas flags once during each school day. It's not known if any other state requires students to pledge to both country and state. But I doubt it.

There's nothing trivial about Texas, and yet it's filled with trivia; it's a gold mine of random bits, all of which contribute to the allure of state. No book can completely capture all of the interesting things about such a state, and in the end, all I can think of are the things left unwritten. We've left out lots of information, brushed over entire areas, not even addressed a tenth of the trivia in the Lone Star State—it's to be expected. So I apologize right now to the dozens of people who gave me engaging trivia that we simply ran out of room for.

Texas—it's bigger than life, fraught with myth, filled with ardent, true believers. I'm one of them. Texan first, last and always.

WHAT'S THE BIG DEAL IN TEXAS? SIZE.

In Texas, it's all about size, and that size is BIG. This is a state that revels in having the biggest everything: the biggest hair; the biggest belt buckles; the biggest boots; the biggest highway system; the biggest church. Although it's not the biggest state, you'd never guess that from talking to natives.

So how big is it, really? If you added up the land area of Connecticut, Maine, Massachusetts, New Hampshire, Rhode Island, Vermont, New York, Pennsylvania, Ohio and Illinois, Texas would be larger. In fact, 41 counties in Texas are each larger than Rhode Island.

Here's another way to measure it. If you were to clip along the edges of Texas on a U.S. map and flip it up, the Rio Grande Valley would reach Canada. Flip it to the west, and it would nearly reach the Pacific Ocean. Flip it to the east, and you're at the Atlantic. So in terms of the 48 contiguous states, it's by far the biggest one on the map. With all that space, it only made sense to fill it with big things.

OFFICIALLY TEXAS

The Name Game

Tejas, tayshas, texias, thecas, techan, teysas, techas and texas—all are versions of a Hasinais Native American word meaning "friends" or "allies." The Hasinais lived in the eastern portion of what is now Texas, and although they didn't use the abovementioned terms to refer to themselves or the land in which they lived, the terms were frequently used as a greeting loosely translated as "Hello, friend."

Scholars aren't in agreement on when the term texas first transitioned from a greeting to the name of a state. Spanish explorers and settlers first used the term to refer to the friendly founders of the land. Eventually, texas was elevated to refer to the place, Texas.

Go Figure
It's no wonder then, that Texas' motto is "Friendship." It was officially adopted as such in 1930.

Nickname

Before Texas officially became Texas, it was referred to as the Lone Star State. It acquired this name after a flag bearing a single star led a series of expeditions to the area. The single-star theme continued to the early days of the Republic of Texas, and some people believed that the star represented one of two ideologies: the desire to achieve statehood in the United States, or the status as Mexico's one and only state. Either way, the theme continued throughout history and is now firmly embedded in the state as its nickname.

Flying High

Continuing on the Lone Star State theme, a single star and the colors red (for bravery), white (for strength) and blue (for loyalty) make up the Texas state flag. The design for the flag was first approved in 1839, when it was adopted as the national flag of the Republic of Texas. It was later officially adopted as the state flag on December 29, 1845, when Texas became the country's 28th state.

Great Journey for a Great Seal

To say the Great Seal of Texas has evolved over the years is perhaps an understatement. The first seal to be used in official proceedings was a single five-pointed star, which was adopted on March 2, 1836, after the Republic of Texas declared independence from Mexico. By December of that year, Sam Houston—who was president of the republic by then—declared that "for the future, the national seal of this republic shall consist of a single star, with the letters 'Republic of Texas' circular on said seal, which seal shall also be circular." By 1839, another modification was added: a live oak branch representing strength and an olive branch representing peace. Of course, by 1845, when Texas became a state, the word "Republic" was changed to reflect that. And while the basic design remained the same, there were slight alterations throughout the years until 1992, when the Secretary of State formally adopted today's official seal.

Sing Out Loud!

Texas, our Texas! All hail the mighty State!
Texas, our Texas! So wonderful, so great!
Boldest and grandest, Withstanding ev'ry test;
O Empire wide and glorious, You stand supremely blest.

"Texas, Our Texas," words by Marsh and Gladys Yoakum Wright and music by William J. Marsh, was adopted as the Texas state song in 1929.

Inspired by a Flower

Of course, Texans appreciate the fine arts—and their state flower—so much that the state also designated an official flower song. Written by Julia D. Booth and Lora C. Crockett, "Bluebonnets" received the designation on March 21, 1933.

DID YOU KNOW?

Texas adopted the idea of naming an official state musician on September 1, 2001. However, that position has remained vacant for several years. Some people argue that Willie Nelson would be the obvious choice.

An Artist's Haven?

It appears that Texas has a fondness for its artists. In a list of state symbols, emblems and mascots, three designations are made for artists. Kid Cardona was the first to be recognized on April 15, 1997, when he was named the state's official caricature artist. On June 3, 1997, two other artists were honored: Carl Rice Embrey was named the state's official two-dimensional media artist, and Edd Hayes was named the state's official three-dimensional media artist.

Special Forces

The Commemorative Air Force (also known as the Confederate Air Force) was named Texas' official air force in 1989. The "air force" is in reality a non-profit, volunteer-run organization whose goal is to collect, restore to flying condition and maintain one of every aircraft that flew during World War II. The collection began with the purchase of a Curtiss P-40 Warhawk in 1951. Today, of the 145 aircraft located at the CAF site, based in the Midland International Airport, 100 are in flying condition. In fact, they've starred in a state anti-litter television commercial and often fly over parades and other special events.

Odd and Original

Since the first 20 head of cattle were gathered in 1941, Texas has been the only state in the country that maintains a state-owned herd. Today, about 100 head, which make up the Texas official state longhorn herd, are cared for within several Texas parks.

Other State Symbols and Emblems

☛ The mockingbird was named Texas' official state bird in 1927.

☛ Texas has designated three official state mammals: small, large and flying. The armadillo was named the state's official small mammal on June 16, 1995, partly because it migrated into the area at roughly the same time settlers started exploring the land. The longhorn was designated the state's official large mammal on May 17, 1969. And the Mexican free-tailed bat was named the state's official flying mammal on May 25, 1995.

☛ The Guadalupe bass, a member of the sunfish far~~~
named Texas' official state fish on May 22, 1989.
this distinction partly because the species is unique to the
state.

☛ On May 28, 1993, the Texas horned lizard was chosen as
the official state reptile.

☛ It's believed Texas is the birthplace of the monarch butterfly, and the state takes the issue of protecting these beautiful creatures very seriously. Abilene Zoological Gardens was
the first official monarch sanctuary along the eastern migra-
tion path. So it's a good fit that the monarch butterfly is the
state's official insect. It was so named on June 6, 1995.

☛ Back in 1901, the *Lupinus subcarnosus* variety of bluebonnet
was first designated as the state flower. In 1971, the *Lupinus
texensis* and all other varieties of bluebonnet were added to
that designation.

☛ Because bluebonnets are so prolific in Texas, it's a no-brainer
that the state has a few designations in the bluebonnet category. Ennis was named Texas' Bluebonnet City and the home
of the official Bluebonnet Trail on June 18, 1997. That same
day, the Chappell Hill Bluebonnet Festival was named the
state's official bluebonnet festival.

☛ It appears that a number of items received official designation on June 18, 1997. That was also the day cotton was
named the state's official fiber and fabric. It only makes sense,
since the state's cotton production is the highest in the country. Texas grows about 25 percent—or 5.4 million bails—of
the nation's total cotton.

☛ Pecan trees are quite prolific in Texas, so it's no wonder the
pecan was named the state's official nut on June 16, 2001.

☛ The pecan was designated the official state tree in 1919.

☛ Recognized for its rugged versatility, beauty and contributions to the landscape, cuisine, and character of Texas, the prickly pear cactus was named the official state plant on May 25, 1995.

☛ On April 12, 1971, sideoats gramma was named the state grass.

☛ On June 18, 1997, the crape myrtle was named the Texas state shrub, making Texas the only state with such a designation.

☛ 'Ruby-Sweet,' 'Rio Star' and 'Flame' are all varieties of the Texas red grapefruit. This citrus favorite was named the Texas state fruit in 1993.

☛ The onion (historically considered a symbol of eternity because of its many circular rings), appears to be the center of a lot of discussion in Texas. The sweet onion was named the state's official vegetable on May 7, 1997.

☛ Hot and spicy! It's one way to describe a Texas chili, and the way it gets its zest is with its secret ingredient: jalapeño peppers. The jalapeño was named the state's official pepper on May 10, 1995.

☛ Of course, the native chiltepin pepper, which grows wild in Texas, couldn't be left out altogether. On June 18, 1995, it was named the state's official native pepper.

☛ Blame it on its Mexican roots, but the official Texas state dish is the hot and spicy chili. It was so named in 1977.

☛ The Brachiosaur sauropod, Pleurocoelus, a 50-foot-long, plant-eating giant once thought to roam Dinosaur Valley State Park in north-central Texas, was honored with the title of official state dinosaur on June 3, 1998.

☞ Texas blue topaz was named the state's official gemstone on March 26, 1969. That same day, petrified palmwood was named the official state stone.

☞ Years later, in 1977, the Lone Star cut—a specific way to cut gemstones—was named the official gemstone cut.

☞ The lightning whelk, an elegant and elaborate seashell, was named the state shell on April 22, 1987, thanks in part to a longstanding resident of Texas, Mildred Tate. She died just three years after the dedication.

☞ In 1979, four separate productions were named Texas' official state plays: *The Lone Star*, *Texas*, *Beyond the Sundown* and *Fandangle*.

☞ The USS *Texas* was named the state ship on June 16, 1995.

☞ Texas isn't unique when it comes to the designation of its official folk dance. Along with numerous other sister states, Texas recognized the square dance in 1991.

☞ Football might be a fan favorite for sports lovers in Texas, but it's rodeo that's earned the title of official state sport. It was so adopted on June 18, 1997.

☞ In recognition of all kinds of musicians, from cowboys sitting around a campfire and strumming a few tunes to teenagers knocking out a beat in their parents' garage, the guitar is recognized as the official state musical instrument of Texas. It was so named on June 18, 1997.

☞ The Tejano Music Hall of Fame in Alice was designated the state music hall of fame on September 1, 2001.

AVERAGES AND EXTREMES

It's Like It's Own Country

A state the size of Texas has a variety of geographic influences, so climate and weather conditions can be quite different from one corner to the next. There are three major climatic types: continental, mountain and modified marine.

Climate in the High Plains areas located in the northernmost portion of the state and along the west boundary to the mountains is considered continental steppe. A wide range of weather-related phenomena, such as extreme daily high and low temperatures, characterize this climate type.

The mountain climate is localized in the far western reaches of the state, around the Guadalupe, Davis and Chisos mountains of the Trans-Pecos region.

The remaining, and largest, portion of the state experiences a modified marine climate, which is largely influenced by proximity to the Gulf of Mexico.

On Average

Texas boasts an average high temperature of 77.3°F and an average low temperature of 55°F.

Let it Rain, Let it Snow

The average annual precipitation in Texas varies greatly, depending on location.

City	Average Annual Rainfall	Average Annual Snowfall
El Paso	7.8 inches	5.4 inches
Amarillo	19.6 inches	16.2 inches
Dallas/Fort Worth	33.7 inches	3.2 inches
Houston*	42.0 inches	0.2 inches
Port Arthur Beaumont	57.2 inches	0.3 inches
Corpus Christi	30.1 inches	0.0 inches
Laredo	24.1 inches	0.0 inches

*Also the lightning strikes capital of the state.

Compared to the Rest

Texas does not make the top 10 when it comes to having a city listed as exhibiting the most or least weather variety, but some Texas cities top the charts when it comes to having some of the nation's most extreme weather conditions.

☛ El Paso is listed as the ninth driest city in the country, recording an average annual precipitation of 7.82 inches.

Brownsville and Corpus Christi both make it on the charts, listed as the sixth and ninth hottest cities in the nation, respectively. Brownsville's average annual temperature is 73.6°F, and Corpus Christi's is 72.1°F.

☛ El Paso places fifth when it comes to the nation's sunniest cities, with an 83 percent average possibility of sunshine.

☛ Texas shows twice when it comes to the nation's windiest cities. With average annual wind speeds of about 13.5 miles per hour, Amarillo ranks third, while Lubbock is in 10th spot with average annual wind speeds of about 12.4 miles per hour.

☛ Port Arthur is listed as the third most humid city in the country, with an average relative humidity of 77.5 percent. Corpus Christi is in seventh spot with 76 percent, and Houston is in 10th with 75 percent.

☛ El Paso is fifth in the nation once again when it comes to the country's least humid cities. El Paso's average relative humidity is 42.5 percent.

Extreme Texas Weather Statistics

☛ The all-time low of –23°F has occurred twice in recorded history: in Tulia on February 12, 1899, and in Seminole on February 8, 1933. The coldest overall winter is said to be the winter of 1898–99.

☛ The all-time high of 120°F has also occurred twice in recorded history: in Seymour on August 12, 1936, and in Monahans on June 28, 1994.

☛ The strongest sustained winds have been recorded at 145 miles per hour at two locations but both on the same day, during Hurricane Carla on September 11, 1961. However, their directionality was different, with the wind coming in

from the southeast at Matagorda and from the northeast
in Port Lavaca.

☛ The highest peak gusts have been recorded at 180 miles per
hour during Hurricane Celia on August 3, 1970, in the
Aransas Pass.

☛ The wettest year in Texas, overall, was 1919, with 41.9 inches
of precipitation recorded.

☛ The driest year in Texas, overall, was 1917, with 14.3 inches
of precipitation recorded.

☛ The wettest year for a city in Texas was recorded in
Clarksville in 1873. A total of 109.4 inches of precipitation
fell that year.

☛ The driest year for a city in Texas was recorded in Presidio
in 1956. Less than two inches of precipitation—1.64 inches
to be exact—fell that year.

☛ The largest accumulation of precipitation to fall in Texas in
a 24-hour period occurred on August 4, 1978. That's when
Albany recorded 29.1 inches of precipitation. However, at
least one estimate challenges that figure. An unofficial
claim of 43 inches collected in Alvin on July 25–26, 1979,
was made during Tropical Storm Claudette.

EXTREME TEXAS WEATHER EVENTS

The Sky is Falling

Farmers everywhere dread the thought of an impending hailstorm, but a review of Texas weather history locates the majority of high-impact hailstorms in major cities. The worst hailstorm on record occurred on May 5, 1995, in Dallas–Fort Worth. Ironically considered a "perfect storm," conditions were right for some of the most extreme weather conditions residents in the area had ever experienced. The end result saw baseball-sized hail falling in some locations of downtown Fort Worth and flash flooding in Dallas. In the end, 19 deaths, 109 injuries and about $2 billion in damage were reported. Following is a list of other significant hailstorms.

- ☞ The High Plains storm of August 24, 1979, cost $200 million in damage, mainly to area crops.

- ☞ Forty-eight people were injured in the May 10, 1996, hailstorm of Howard County.

- ☞ About $800 million in damage were reported after a supercell thunderstorm propelled baseball-sized hail and five tornadoes throughout 16 counties on April 5, 2003.

DID YOU KNOW?

The city of San Angelo owes its existence to the flash flood of August 23–24, 1882. Heavy rains resulting from a thunderstorm caused a flood in the town of Ben Ficklin, which was then the seat of Tom Green County. An estimated 45 people were killed, and the town was destroyed. When it came to rebuilding, the remaining townsfolk moved to higher ground, and Santa Angela was born. The next year, the post office changed the name to San Angelo.

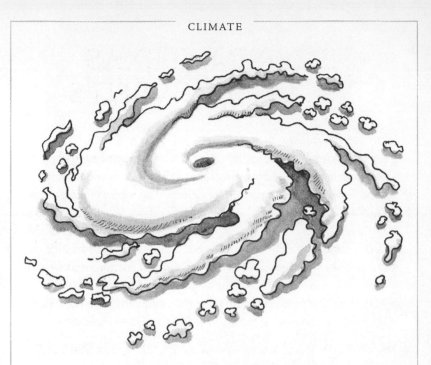

Hurricane Headlines

Of the hurricanes to hit Texas, the one that hit Galveston on September 8, 1900, is said by most sources to be the most damaging and deadly. A large portion of the city was destroyed, and as many as 10,000 people were killed, making the Category 4 storm the worst natural disaster in the history of the United States in terms of loss of life. Economically, Katrina has had the greatest impact, strictly in terms of cost. Of course, other hurricanes and tropical storms have also had a devastating impact on Texas.

- ☛ Corpus Christi was hit with a Category 4 hurricane on September 14, 1919. The death toll topped 284.

- ☛ Galveston was again hit by a devastating storm in August 1915. Despite all the precautions taken following the 1900 disaster, 275 people died.

- ☛ Although Hurricane Claudette didn't officially make hurricane status, the storm in July 1979 still managed to cause about $750 million in damage in the Houston area.

☛ Hurricane Carla formed on September 3, 1961, and raged for 13 days before eventually petering out. Even though it is considered by many sources to be the strongest hurricane ever recorded to hit Texas, only a relatively low 41 deaths were recorded.

☛ A Category 3 hurricane hit Alicia in August 1983, injuring 1800 people and causing $3 billion in damage.

☛ Tropical Storm Allison, which hit southeast Texas on June 4–10, 2001, is considered one of the most expensive storms to hit the state, resulting in $5.2 billion in damage.

☛ Hurricane Rita touched down on the Texas-Louisiana border in September 2005. The Category 3 hurricane cost 119 lives and is among the nation's billion-dollar weather events, racking up $16 billion in damage.

DID YOU KNOW?

"Carla" was retired as a hurricane name after the 1961 event. Carla was the first hurricane to be filmed and shown on national television. Wharton native Dan Rather, a cub journalist at the time, reported on the event, setting the standard for television storm reporting.

Tornado Alley

It may not come as a surprise that the Tornado Alley part of Texas tends to overlap the Bible Belt of Texas. There's a whole lot of praying in those storm shelters. Here are some of the more dramatic storms to hit the Lone Star state.

Everything Looks Fine...

An F5 tornado struck the town of Jarrell in 1997. The twister was three-quarters of mile wide and tracked across the ground for 7.6 miles. Twenty-seven people were killed (out of 131 residents), and an entire subdivision was wiped off the map—all 38 houses and several mobile homes were vaporized. The first sheriff's deputy on the scene was unfamiliar with the area and thought there had been no damage at all, because there was literally no debris from the houses that had been there. Even sewer and water pipes had been sucked out of the ground.

20-Year Record
An F4 tornado hit a heavily populated part of Wichita Falls on April 10, 1979. It left 20,000 people homeless, killed 42 people (25 in vehicles) and caused $400 million in damage—a U.S. record that wasn't topped by a single tornado until the F5 in Oklahoma City came through 20 years later.

But Gee, the View Was Incredible!

Tornadoes don't just limit themselves to rural parts of Texas. Downtown Fort Worth was hit with an F2 twister in 2000 that destroyed a number of buildings. The 454-foot-tall Bank One Tower, heavily damaged in the tornado, was slated for destruction, which would have made it the tallest structure in North America to be demolished. For reasons that remain unclear, the building's demolition was postponed repeatedly. Eventually, it became known as the "Plywood Skyscraper" because of all the wood used to cover blown-out windows. It has since been converted to condominiums.

Record Holder

The deadliest tornado in Texas history was the F5 that struck Waco on May 11, 1953. With wind speeds of over 300 miles per hour, a funnel cloud two blocks wide hit downtown. One car was crushed to 18 inches in height, and a six-story furniture store crumbled to the ground. In the end, 114 people were killed—no deadlier single tornado has struck the U.S. since.

JUST THE FACTS

On the Map

Texas is located in the south-central part of the United States. It is bordered on the southeast by the Gulf of Mexico and on the southwest by Mexico, while New Mexico borders Texas to the west, Oklahoma to the north and Arkansas and Louisiana to the east.

The Texas Almanac divides Texas into four main physical regions: the Gulf Coastal Plains, Interior Lowlands, Great Plains and the Basin and Range Province.

Overall Size

Texas is the second largest state in the U.S., covering an amazing 268,581 square miles. Of that number, 261,797 square miles, or 97.5 percent, is land, and 6784 square miles, or 2.5 percent, is water. Texas could accommodate Connecticut, Maine, Massachusetts, New Hampshire, Rhode Island, Vermont, New York, Pennsylvania, Ohio, West Virginia and Virginia simultaneously within its borders. The largest state in the U.S. is Alaska, with 656,424 square miles. California lags considerably behind in third spot, with 163,707 square miles.

High Point
Guadalupe Peak is the Texas high spot at an elevation of 8749 feet.

Center Point
The average elevation in Texas is 1700 feet.

Lowest Point
The Gulf of Mexico is the lowest elevation in Texas, at sea level.

Coastline Measurements
There are 367 miles of coastline where Texas meets the Gulf of Mexico.

Major Waterways

Three-quarters of Texas is surrounded by water, either by the Gulf of Mexico or by rivers along neighboring state borders. Locals often consider it a jewel along the "Third Coast." As well, Texas can boast about 41 major waterways and another 44 seasonal and restrictive waterways. The 10 longest rivers of the state are listed below. Each of these rivers empties into the Gulf of Mexico.

☞ Rio Grande: 1250 miles in Texas (1896 miles in total)

☞ Colorado River: 862 miles in Texas (and in total)

☞ Brazos River: 840 miles in Texas (1280 miles in total)

☞ Red River: 680 miles in Texas (1360 miles in total)

☞ Trinity River: 550 miles in Texas (and in total)

☞ Pecos River: 500 miles in Texas (926 miles in total)

☞ Neches River: 416 miles in Texas (and in total)

☞ Sabine River: 360 miles in Texas (555 miles in total)

☞ Nueces River: 315 miles in Texas (and in total)

☞ Canadian River: 200 miles in Texas (760 miles in total)

Lack of Lakes

A weekend at the beach in Texas likely means a trip to the coast or a visit to one of the state's many rivers. Lakes in Texas are typically small; the largest natural lake in Texas is Caddo Lake, although it has been artificially raised as a result of damming in 1914 and again in 1971. On average, the lake is 8 to 10 feet deep, but it manages to provide habitat to 71 varieties of fish species.

 All but one of Texas' 77 lakes are artificial. They are actually reservoirs, not lakes, and combined with ground water stores they hold 25 million acre-feet of water. Since the lakes are often constructed around low areas with substantial rivers, there are some interesting things under all that water. Canyon Lake in the Texas Hill Country has two towns at the bottom of it that were bought up and abandoned when the dam was built. Lake Grapevine has a line of dump trucks that were trapped when a rainstorm came through and flooded the area after they closed the dam—but before they got the trucks out.

Parks Galore

Texas has 115 state parks, covering more than 600,000 acres. Statistics show that more than $44 billion is spent on recreation in these areas by the millions of tourists who visit each year. There are also 12 national parks, including Big Bend, one of the last remaining "wild corners" of the U.S.

Along with its parks, Texas has named five state forests, occupying 7314 acres: Fairchild State Forest is made up of 2740 acres originally owned by the Texas State Prison System; Jones State Forest's 1725 acres are home to the endangered red-cockaded woodpecker; Kirby State Forest's 600 acres were donated by a lumberman; Masterson State Forest, though 519 acres, is hard to find and rarely shown on maps; and Siecke Rate Forest is made up of 1722 acres, with fishing permitted.

Capital City

*..*fourth largest city in Texas, is the state capital. It was founded in 1835 and originally named Waterloo. Its name was changed to Austin in 1838 in honor of Stephen Fuller Austin, founder of the Republic of Texas.

 When it comes to the state with the largest number of counties, Texas has earned bragging rights hands down. I'd be willing to bet that even the most studious student (or ardent politician) couldn't name them all 254 of them.

County Curiosities

☞ When it comes to size, Brewster County is the largest, with 6193 square miles.

☞ Pecos County is the second largest county in Texas. Its population, however, is quite modest; according to 2000 U.S. Census figures, 16,809 residents share 4765 square miles of space. It also seems to be quite a peaceful population, with not a single murder reported in 2000.

☞ Covering roughly 147 square miles, Rockwall County is the smallest county in Texas. It is named after the largely underground rock wall formation that crosses the entire county.

☞ Lubbock County's moniker "Diamond in the West" has been attributed to the fact that the entire county was once a vast lake.

☞ Bosque County (pronounced "boss-kee" and meaning "wooded") was so named by Spanish explorers for the natural forested beauty of the area.

☞ Harris County is the most populated in the state, with 3,693,050 residents, based on 2005 estimates.

☛ The Davis Mountains are the highest mountain range located entirely within Texas, and much of that range can be found in Jeff Davis County. Archaeological research in the area has uncovered more than 1200 arrow points and other evidence of occupation by a prehistoric civilization dating back to 1000 AD.

☛ Hays County calls itself one of Texas' fastest-growing counties.

☛ Black gold was first discovered in Anderson County in 1881, and the first rig made it to the area in 1902.

☛ Oil was first discovered in Freestone County in 1916. By the end of 2004, the county had recovered 44,889,337 barrels of oil.

☛ What was once a land of oil rigs and rodeo, Tarrant County has welcomed the cosmopolitan, big city life and today, proudly describes itself as "the perfect mix of cowboys and culture."

☛ Jones County was named after Anson Jones. He was the last president of the Republic of Texas before it became a state.

DID YOU KNOW?

If you're a little leery about living near areas prone to volcanoes and earthquakes, Texas might be the perfect state for you. The state has no active or dormant volcanoes and very few earthquakes. The most active part of the state, when it comes to seismic activity, is the Big Bend area.

UNIQUE GEOGRAPHY

Natural Wonder

Padre Island National Seashore near Corpus Christi covers 130,454 acres. It's considered the longest remaining undeveloped stretch of barrier island in the world. Almost half of the bird species—380 different varieties—found in North America have been known to frequent the area.

Natural Monolith

Enchanted Rock State Natural Area, located near Fredericksburg, occupies 1643.5 acres of parkland. Its major attraction is a large, granite rock that protrudes 425 feet above ground and covers 640 acres of the park. Enchanted Rock was initially an underground rock formation, but it has been uncovered through years of erosion. It is thought to be one of the nation's largest batholiths. It's also a favorite place for local rock climbing enthusiasts.

One-of-a-Kind Formations

Guadalupe Mountains National Park near Van Horn is well known as the location of Guadalupe Peak, the highest point in Texas. The park also boasts one of the world's largest marine fossil reefs, drawing geologists from across the globe to study its formation. Throughout history, the mountain range, and in particular El Capitan's rock face, represented a compass point of sorts to pioneers and travelers through the area. Visitors will likely notice how past civilizations marked their journey through the area by the many pictographs found throughout the park.

What Is It, Really?

The meteor crater 10 miles southwest of Odessa has been a source of mystery since its discovery by area rancher Julius D. Henderson in 1892. The circular depression, which measures 100 feet deep and between 500 and 650 feet across. The general consensus is that the depression was formed by a meteor shower between 20,000 and 75,000 years ago. Some scientists believe the meteor is entombed below the crater surface, but attempts recover it, or even prove it still exists, have been unsuccessful.

Where Water Sits

For a millennium, people living in the arid area outside El Paso used the rock basins of Hueco Tanks as a natural supply of water. Large, natural rock basins, or *huecos*, trapped rainwater for people who, while they were there, contributed hundreds of pictographs. There are more than 200 face designs or "masks" left by the prehistoric Jornada Mogollon culture. Apaches, Kiowas and earlier tribes left their marks as well, telling of their adventures in this western corner of Texas. The rocks themselves look like huge lumps of clay tossed down on a wide space in the desert. These days, there's a great deal of concern about the condition of the pictographs, which, after weathering thousands of years of people, animals and torrential rains, are crumbling under increased traffic to the park.

PROTECTION FOR ALL

Forced Adaptation

Not all of the 97,000 acres that make up Big Thicket National Preserve are populated by flora and fauna native to the area. Scientists believe that many of the 1000-plus varieties of flowering plants, 85 species of trees, 60 shrubs and assorted ferns, orchids and insect-eating plants currently found there were transported into the area during the last ice age.

Recognition that this area needed protection from oil and lumber companies took place fairly early on when R.E. Jackson formed the East Texas Big Thicket Association in 1927. Initially it was hoped that 400,000 acres would be set aside for protection, but it wasn't until 1974 that the initial 84,500 acres were established. It's known as "America's Ark."

DID YOU  **KNOW?**

The pitcher plant and sundew, two varieties of carnivorous, insect-eating plants, can be found along the Sundew Trail in Big Thicket National Preserve.

ENDANGERED SPECIES

Unique Tree

Texas is home to a very small number of Hinckley's oak trees still in existence. The desert scrub evergreens grow primarily in arid areas of Brewster and Presidio counties, including Monahans Sandhills State Park and the Chihuahuan Desert at elevations of about 4500 feet. While they grow to a height of only about four feet, their roots descend as deep as 90 feet, stabilizing the sand dunes they call home. According to Texas Parks and Wildlife statistics from 2002, there are only about 10 populations of the species still in existence. While human infringement and animal grazing are always a threat to depleting populations of rare plant species, the biggest danger to the survival of the Hinckley's oak is a change in Texas climate, which has become more dry and arid over the last 10,000 years.

Very Fishy

The paddlefish, or spoonbill, may have been part of a commercial fishery at one time, but today it is a protected species. The unique fish, which commonly grows to a weight of between 40 and 60 pounds, has a long, sword-like snout and feeds on freshwater plankton.

Whopping Recovery

A one-time rare species of whooping crane could credit its comeback to the efforts of the Aransas National Wildlife Refuge Complex, located near Austwell. The 115,000 acres of protected parkland provide winter habitat to this rare crane variety that, in 1941, with a population of just 15 birds, was on the verge of extinction. The snow white adult bird, with its black bill and black-tipped wings that span a full seven feet, measures five feet tall, making it the tallest bird on the continent. The only wild flock typically arrives in Aransas from its summer home in Canada's Wood Buffalo National Park by December. The population of the species is monitored each year, with a September 2006 count putting its numbers at about 354, not including those being raised in captivity.

Ribbit, Ribbit

Once considered little more than a pest and pretty much exterminated in the city of Houston, the toad bearing the city's name is considered an endangered amphibian species. The purple-gray Houston toad, which at adulthood measures between two and three and a half inches, was first identified in the 1940s and was originally found in 12 counties throughout the state. Today, its range has been significantly reduced, and the toad has been confirmed in only three of those counties.

Cat Country

The Laguna Atascosa National Wildlife Refuge near Rio Hondo is home to several endangered animal and bird species. Among these protected creatures are the ocelot (which is easily recognizable by its leopard-like spots) and the jaguarondi (a close relative of the puma)—both powerful, beautiful wild cats whose main threat is loss of habitat.

GONE BUT NOT FORGOTTEN

Flying Giants

Douglas Lawson discovered the remains of a 65-million-year-old pterodactyl in Big Bend National Park in 1971. The find is still considered the largest of its kind ever unearthed.

Mass Burial

The Waco Mammoth Site can so far boast 24 mammoths uncovered. They are part of the largest known herd that died from a single cause. Scientists believe the mammoths, grazing near the river, drowned when the riverbank gave way as the result of a heavy thunderstorm about 28,000 years ago.

Hill Country Dinosaur Footprints

The Texas Hill Country has two excellent dinosaur footprint sites. On the banks of the Blanco River, there are clear imprints made by dinosaurs just at the water's edge. At first glance, the prints look like indentations carved by erosion, but careful inspection will reveal the shape of the foot and toe imprints.

The second footprint site is at the Boerne Lake Spillway. You can see indentations in the rock layer, which are actually two separate sets of dinosaur tracks. The larger set of tracks was made by a bipedal dinosaur, possibly a theropod. Smaller prints, also made by a bipedal dinosaur, cross the larger ones.

Unfortunately, the tracks are not accessible to the public, but you can view casts of the prints at the Cibolo Nature Center.

BY THE NUMBERS

One, Two, Three...
The population of Texas, based on the 2000 U.S. Census, was 20,851,820 (2005 estimates put that number at closer to 22,859,968), making it the second most populated state in the country. If you spread that number out over the entire state, it's the equivalent of 79.6 persons per square mile.

Population Through the Years

Census Year	Population
1850	212,592
1860	604,215
1870	818,579
1880	1,591,749
1890	2,235,527
1900	3,048,710
1950	7,711,194
1980	14,229,191
2000	20,851,820

Who's Counting Whom?
Official population statistics will list San Antonio as larger than Dallas, but as a metropolitan area, Dallas is nearly three times as large. San Antonio often ranks about 37th as a media market, while Dallas ranks seventh and Houston ranks 10th. What's the reason for the discrepancy? The City of Dallas doesn't absorb its suburbs in the same way as the City of San Antonio does. So the official population of Dallas doesn't include a few million people who most ad executives consider locals.

Most Populated Cities

As the nation's second most populated state, it's no surprise that Texas' three most populated cities also rank among the top 10 most populated cities in the country. Here are Texas' six most populated cities in descending order based on 2004 census data:

City	Population	Country Ranking
Houston	2,016,582	4th
San Antonio	1,256,509	7th
Dallas	1,213,825	9th
Austin	690,252	16th
Fort Worth	624,067	19th
El Paso	598,590	21st

DID YOU  KNOW?

Men outnumber women in Bee County, where only 39.5 percent of the population is female, according to 2004 census estimates.

TEXAS MELTING POT

Mother Tongue

Texas may have a lot of special designations, but an official language is not among them. American English is the most common language used in the political and legal realms. Spanish, a close second, is the preferred language of about one-third of Texas' population. Vietnamese and Chinese have recently risen to the status of the third and fourth most popular languages, replacing German and French in the process.

Ethnic Diversity

The following statistics are based on 2004 estimates from the U.S. Census Bureau.

Race	Percentage of Population
White (non-Hispanic)	49.2
Hispanic or Latino	35.1
Black	11.7
Asian/Pacific Islander	3.3
American Indian/Alaskan Native	0.7
Persons with two or more ethnic backgrounds	1.0

Population by Ancestry

North America is a mosaic of various ethnic ancestries. The five most prominent in Texas are Mexican, at 25.3 percent of the population; German, at 10.9 percent; African American, at 10.5 percent; English, at 7.2 percent; and Scotch-Irish, at 7.2 percent.

TEJANO

Music, Food and More!

Tejano (Spanish for Texan) is the name given to the music and culture and often the people of Hispanic descent who grew out of the soil of the state, literally. Born from the ranching and farming culture, by 1835, Tejanos were distinct from Mexicans. From the start they did not consider themselves Mexicans; in fact, they fought for Texas Independence from Mexico. They had their own clothing, music, customs and, most importantly, their own food.

Pass the Heat, Please

Foreigners (as Texans refer to people from out of state) will call the food Mexican, but for anyone who has had single meal in Mexico City, it's clear that Tex-Mex is intensely different. Tex-Mex uses more beef, beans and spices. Traditional Mexican food is not as starch-based—or as hot. The official state snack, chips and salsa, however, can be found on either side of the border. Texans are particularly proud of their own brands of salsa, which fill local grocery store shelves. For years, a San Antonio salsa maker poked fun at a national competitor whose product was made in New York. "New York City?" said a cowboy in their TV commercial. "Get a rope."

Tex-Mex cuisine originals include crispy tacos, crispy chalupas, chili con queso, chili con carne, fajitas and even nachos.

Hola and Good Morning!

The Spanish spoken is Texas is often called "Spanglish" or "Tex-Mex," but whatever it is, anyone who speaks it knows it would sound completely foreign in Mexico City or Spain. Using what linguists call code switching, Spanglish speakers will use an interesting mix of English and Spanish.

A Spanglish Conversation:

Sonia: *Hola*, good morning, Rubén. *¿Como estas?* (Hi, good morning, Ruben. How are you?)

Rubén: Good, good. *¿Y tú?* (Good, good. And you?)

Sonia: *Bien, pero* tired. (Good, but tired.)

Rubén: *¿Por que?* What happened? (Why? What happened?)

Sonia: I was working on *mija's aplicación para colegio* all night. (I was working on my daughter's college application all night.)

The Call of the Accordion

Tejano music, like the food, is not Mexican or American. Because Texas was initially so remote from Mexico, the culture developed more ties with Louisiana than Mexico. So in Tejano music you'll find Cajun, rock and roll, R&B, Mexican and country music influences. Tejano music (often broken down into conjunto, orchestra and modern) features accordions, electric guitars, bajo sexto (a type of 12 string guitar) and even a brass section for some bands. Famous Tejano performers include Selena (murdered by the president of her fan club, she was the first Tejano artist to receive a Grammy), Emilio Navaira, La Mafia, Flaco Jimenez and Little Joe.

GERMAN INFLUENCE

Could You Spell That, Please?

Much of the Texas Hill Country was settled by German immigrants, something that becomes clear when you read a list of community names in the area: Fredericksburg, Luckenbach, New Braunfels, Gruene and Castroville. The town of Biegel, in Fayette County, was thought to be the first German settlement in all of Texas. Today, nothing remains of this community, which is currently located at the bottom of Fayette Power Plant Lake.

From the Gardens to the New World
Johann Friedrich Ernst's father had been a professional gardener in the Grand Duchy of Oldenburg in northwestern Germany. But Ernst wasn't interested in hoeing in his father's footsteps. After a stint in the military, he got a job as the clerk in the post office in Oldenberg, married and had seven children. In 1829, he took his family and left for New York. Once gone, he was accused of embezzling a large amount of money from the post office. While he and his family were on their way to settle in Missouri, Ernst learned that large land grants were available to Europeans in Stephen F. Austin's colony in Texas. Ernst got a grant of more than 4000 acres in the northwest corner of Austin County. It formed the nucleus of the German Belt. His was the first German family in Texas.

Come On Over!

Never underestimate the power of a little publicity. Ernst must have taken a few marketing courses during his time in New York, because his missives about Texas had a tremendous effect. Publicity about Texas in Germany in the 1830s fired up a few petty noblemen, who must have imagined Texas as a place they could rule (a mistake many politicians have since repeated).

Before long, more than 7000 Germans headed for Texas. Some perished in epidemics, many stayed in cities such as Galveston, Houston and San Antonio, and others settled in the rugged Texas Hill Country to form the western end of the German Belt.

We're All the Same...Only Different

Each area of the Hill Country was settled by a different group of Germans: the Llano Valley had stern, teetotaling German Methodists (they renounced dancing and fraternal organizations); the Pedernales Valley had fun-loving, hardworking Lutherans and Catholics (all for drinking and dancing); and the Guadalupe Valley was settled by atheist Germans (descended from intellectual political refugees).

DID YOU KNOW?

New Braunfels only stopped printing its community newspaper, the *Zeitung* (*Zeitung* means "newspaper" in German), in both German and English in 1958, switching to all English. Several section headlines still include the old German name, though; for example, *stammitsch* for the local calendar section, and *vida leben* for the lifestyle section.

Only in Texas

Sprechen sie Texan? Texas German is a unique dialect of German spoken by the descendants of German immigrants who came to Texas around 1830. It's a dying language, largely because the two World Wars made speaking German almost impolite in the U.S. Fortunately, Texas German is being archived by the Texas German Dialect Project at the University of Texas at Austin. Texas German has a bit of Spanish and English melded together, along with its own unique words. For example, airplanes are called *flugzeug* in standard German, which translates to "flying thing." Texas German speakers created the word *luftschiff*, which is based on "airship."

AFRICAN AMERICANS IN TEXAS

Here from the Start
African Americans have been here since the start of European discovery in 1528. Estavanico traveled with Cabeza de Vaca across the territory that would become Texas. Most African Americans, though, would enter the state as slaves, not explorers. After the Civil War, a few thousand African-American Texans took part in cattle drives and became soldiers. Known as Buffalo Soldiers, they took on the Cheyenne, Kiowa, Comanche, Apache, Sioux and Arapaho.

DID YOU KNOW?

In 1860, about 369 slaves lived in Cooke County, representing 10.9 percent of the total population.

100 Years: It's Time for Change

During the Texas centennial of 1936, African Americans made an effort to highlight their contributions to the state. When the celebrations were over, they launched an effort to win citizenship rights and challenged the state's white primary system until they successfully eliminated segregation in graduate and professional schools, setting the stage for national legal and societal victories.

Artistic Influence
In the late 19th and 20th centuries, the influence of African-American culture on Texas came through in the blues and jazz innovators of the time. Some of the most famous were Blind Lemon Jefferson, Huddie (Leadbelly) Ledbetter and Bobbi Humphrey. They planted the seeds that would impact the music of Stevie Ray Vaughn, Buddy Holly and countless others.

TEXAS CZECH

Czech Mate

There are more Czech Americans in Texas than in any other state, possibly as many as 400,000. Although Czech speakers are dwindling in number, a good bit of Texas Czech culture remains strong. When Czech people originally arrived in the state, they looked for farmland. They saw farming as more than a way to make money. For the Czech, farming was a way of life and was important in preserving the tradition of a closely knit family that works together.

Two Famous Texas Czechs

Frederick Lemsky arrived in Texas in 1836 and played the fife in the battle of San Jacinto.

Josef Arnost Bergman is considered the father of Czech immigration. He wrote to his friends in Europe about the opportunities in Texas, stimulating the Bohemian and Moravian immigration. Fayette County was the center of the Czech population in Texas. By the time the Civil War rolled around, 700 Czechs were settled in Texas. By 1910, their numbers were up to over 15,000.

Oompah!

Get out your polka shoes because there's plenty of opportunity to wear down the heels in Texas. A number of Czech festivals are held in the state annually, including Czech Fest in Rosenberg, Czhilispiel in Flatonia, Westfest in West and the National Polka Festival in Ennis. And if you think polka is strictly old school, think again. The Texas-born group Brave Combo has won two Grammys for their unique combination of polka, jazz and rock. The group was the headliner at the 2007 National Polka Festival. Preserving all this liveliness is not being left to chance. In 2004, the first phase of the Texas Czech Heritage and Cultural Center opened in La Grange.

ROADSIDE ATTRACTIONS

Prada, You Say?

If you blink as you drive by, you'll likely think you saw nothing more than a mirage. Then again, you might put on the breaks and turn around, just to be sure. And before you know it, you're gazing into a shop window looking at Prada's 2005 line of fall footwear. Prada Marfa, as this "shop" on U.S. Highway 90 near Marfa and Valentine is called, is actually a minimalist sculpture that is eye-candy only—tempting, but don't touch. There are no operable doors or windows through which to enter the building. It's completely sealed and preserved for all posterity. It does, however, break up the monotony of an otherwise desolate stretch of highway—something Marfa's artists are particularly proud of.

Gotta Beer...Can?

In the late 1960s, Houstonian John Milkovish thought up an innovative way to avoid spending his retirement mowing the lawn. The one-time railroad upholsterer poured concrete over his lawn and inlaid marble, rock, metal—just about any kind of ornate object—into the wet cement, creating an interesting mosaic in the process. It went so well, in fact, that Milkovish moved on to his house, covering the outer walls with beer cans that he'd removed the tops and bottoms from and flattened by slitting them up the sides. For 18 years he drank a six-pack a day and saved nearly 40,000 cans—more than enough flattened pieces of tin to cover his house and have plenty leftover for other projects like metal curtains, mobiles, fences and the like. Milkovish died in 1988, but the house was acquired by the Orange Show Foundation and remains a favorite roadside attraction for folks visiting Houston.

Barbed Tribute

Cattle farmers will likely appreciate this roadside attraction the most. It's apparently the only tribute of its kind to the 1874 invention of barbed wire, which is commonly credited with giving ranchers control of the land. The actual sculpture consists of two 370-pound balls of barbed wire, each perched atop posts made of 125-year-old Kansas limestone. The sculptures, donated by Keller residents Frank and Violet Smith in 1992, currently sit in front of the Devil's Rope Museum in McLean.

Hidalgo is mighty proud to be home to the world's largest killer bee. The 20-foot-long, 10-foot-high killer bee replica was unveiled on December 2, 1992, and one can't help but wonder if the reason for its creation was to give Hidalgo a little protection. You see, Hidalgo's other claim to fame is that it was the first place in the U.S. where the potentially deadly Africanized honeybees were discovered on October 15, 1990. With the world's largest killer bee hanging about the city, one would hope it would pose, at the very least, a fictitious threat to its pesky, living cousins.

Only in Paris?

Paris, Texas, is memorable for several reasons. Known as the "Best Small Town in Texas," its name isn't easily forgettable. Couple that with one of the world's largest replicas of the Eiffel Tower, and it will remain part of you forever. The 65-foot-tall statue might not measure up to its French cousin, but it has a uniquely Texas flavor. In 1998, a large, bright red cowboy hat was added to the top of the monument.

The French Connection

Obviously the French have had an impact on the formation of Texas. The state can not only boast an Eiffel Tower, but a Lourdes as well. A replica of the French shrine, built in 1928, can be found in Rio Grande City.

A Dog's Dream

Beaumont is in mourning. Although it once had bragging rights as the home of the world's largest fire hydrant, it's moved down the ranks a little to third place. The 24-foot, 4500-pound, Dalmatian-spotted fire hydrant gracing the front courtyard of the State Fire Museum of Texas lost its 1999 claim to fame after artist Blue Sky erected a 39-foot, silver version in February 2001 in South Carolina. Later that same year, on July 1, Canada Day, Elm Creek, Manitoba, Canada, also bettered the Beaumont version with a 29.5-foot, red fire hydrant of its own. Either way, Beaumont's Dalmatian variety does deserve special recognition. The monument was made in Disneyland and donated to the town as part of a publicity stunt for the re-release of Disney's hit movie *101 Dalmatians*.

Taking Flight

If you're passing through Austin and forgot about its reputation as home to the largest urban bat population in the world, this should serve as a visual reminder. Artist Dale Whistler designed Night Wing, a rotating, purple bat sculpture, for the city. It stands on the corner of South Congress and Barton Springs Road.

Nosedive

The old adage is true. Build it and they will come—to almost anything! Back in 1974, Stanley Marsh 3 (as in "the third," but he always felt roman numerals were too snobbish), buried 10 vintage Cadillacs nose down on his ranch on Route 66 west of Amarillo. The feat was pulled off with help from the Ant Farm, a San Francisco–based art group, and was meant to represent the "Golden Age of Automobiles." Visitors are always welcome to the famed Cadillac Ranch, and graffiti is encouraged.

MUST-SEE PLACES

The Top Five Attractions in Texas—the Envelope Please
In 2005, the Alamo, the San Antonio River Walk, the San Marcos
Outlet Malls, SeaWorld of Texas (you didn't know there was an
ocean there, did you?) and Six Flags Over Texas were the top five
attractions for non-Texan leisure visitors. So it's history, romance,
shopping and thrills. Sounds about right. Number 30 on the list
was the George Bush Presidential Library, considerably lower than
two zoos and the Fort Worth stockyards. To be fair, it's tough to
compete with longhorns thundering down Main Street.

Ahoy Mates!

Landlubbers with a heart for the sea should check out the Pirate
and Smuggling Museum on the Gulf Coast's Padre Island. The
museum has a seemingly endless display of pirate history,
including grappling hooks, pistols, gunpowder flasks and
tobacco, not to mention officer manuals, newspaper articles featuring stories on apprehended pirates and smugglers, and even
mannequins depicting the fate of these seafaring deviants.

Ron Francis William Dowling gathered the collection in the
1970s. A bit of a pirate in his own right, Dowling was known
to smuggle bicycle tires under his navy uniform during the war.
The items, in high demand and difficult to procure back then,
brought him his beer money. When Dowling died in 2003, his
son John took over and moved the museum from England to
Padre Island, thinking it a good location after learning of that
area's pirate history. The museum, which opened in July 2006,
is open most days from 10:00 AM to 6:00 PM.

Thar' She Blows!
A one-of-a-kind marvel of marine travel restored and open for
visitors is the *Elissa*. Built circa 1877, the tall ship is the focal
point of the Texas Seaport Museum in Galveston. Due for

demolition in 1974, the *Elissa* was rescued and restored, and today it is a National Historic Landmark. Other exhibits at the museum highlight the country's immigration history.

Looking Back, Looking Forward

A visit to the San Jacinto Museum of History, just a 20-minute drive from downtown Houston, offers up a whole lot more than stagnant displays and dusty artifacts. Visitors to this must-see museum are provided with an all-round overview of Texas history—and in more ways than one. The Jesse H. Jones Theater for Texas Studies sets the stage by providing patrons with a 35-minute production on Texas history and the fight for independence on the hour, every hour. Artifacts from various periods of Texas history, from the colonial, Spanish, Mexican and even French, help visitors learn about the various influences on the state's development. The museum itself actually forms the foundation for the 570-foot-tall San Jacinto Monument, the world's tallest memorial column. And a short walk to the nearby battleship *Texas* gives visitors a first-hand look into Texas naval history. Here are a few tidbits on the great battleship *Texas*:

☛ The USS *Texas* was launched on May 18, 1912.

☛ She served in World War I and World War II.

☛ When she was commissioned in 1914, she was considered the most powerful weapon in the world.

☛ Just a few years into service, the *Texas* had mounted anti-aircraft guns and was able to control gunfire with directors and range-keepers, making it the first U.S. battleship able to do so.

☛ By 1919, aircraft were able to take off from the tarmac of the *Texas*—another first for any battleship.

☛ In 1939, it became the first battleship in the U.S. Navy to be equipped with commercial radar.

Out to Sea

The Flagship Hotel in Galveston offers a one-of-a-kind experience. The hotel, which first opened in 1965, was built on concrete posts about 1000 feet out into the Gulf of Mexico. The reasoning behind the architectural decision was to provide guests with a view of the ocean no matter where their room was situated. Talk about considerate!

Historic Replicas

Every museum needs at least one claim to fame that makes it unique and is sure to draw visitors. The Corpus Christi Museum of Science and History has at least two. The *Niña*, *Pinta* and *Santa Maria*—Christopher Columbus' three famous ships—were reproduced in Spain in celebration of the 500th anniversary of Columbus' North American landing. While all three ships were replicated and then sailed to the U.S., visiting several ports before making their way to their permanent resting place in 1993, the *Niña* is moored at the nearby marina and is not open for public tours. The other two, however, are.

First Class Exit

I'm not sure if this would be my first choice for a museum visit, but for folks interested in funerary, the National Museum of Funeral History in Houston is supposedly about as good as it gets. The museum highlights the history of coffin building and country-specific traditions. For example, Ghanaian residents believe a coffin should be shaped in the form of an individual's past occupation. The 12-piece fantasy coffin exhibit boasts coffins carved into the shape of a KLM airliner, a Mercedes Benz, a fish, a canoe, a leopard, a chicken, a bull, a crab, a fish eagle, a lobster, a shallot and a Yamaha outboard motor. The museum opened its doors in October 1992, and its motto says it all: "Any day above ground is a good one."

Transformed

While it may have housed a few unscrupulous scoundrels in its day, the Shackelford County jail doesn't cater to that sort of clientele anymore. Now called the Old Jail Art Center, the building, located in Albany, has been transformed into a gallery featuring all manner of visual arts. The building, which was erected in 1877 at a cost of $9000, was decommissioned as a jail back in 1929 after a more modern facility was built. It was destined for the wrecking ball in 1940 until Robert E. Nail, a local artist and writer, purchased the jail for the grand total of $25 and the lot where it stood for $325. The status of the building continued to evolve over the years. It was listed on the National Register of Historic Places in 1976, and by 1980, it officially opened as the Old Jail Art Center. Today, its 14,000 square feet of space house art, as well as memorabilia highlighting the history of Shackelford County.

All That Money

Folks passing through Fort Worth might want to consider a tour of the U.S. Bureau of Engraving and Printing's Western Currency Facility. Each year the plant, which is one of two such plants in the country, prints 4.5 billion Federal Reserve notes, and visitors can watch as they roll hot off the press from a quarter-mile-long production line.

Big, Hairy Deal

Dallas is home to the Texas Bigfoot Research Center. It was founded in 1999 by Craig Woolheater after a close encounter of the hairy kind. Apparently, Woolheater was driving to Dallas from New Orleans in May 1994 when he came across a large, hairy, two-legged creature. The focus of the organization is to substantiate the existence of Bigfoot through research and by following up on reported sightings.

Going Buggy

A visit to the Cockroach Hall of Fame in Plano means you'll have first-hand information on who, exactly, "Liberoache," "Marilyn Monroach" and even "David Letteroach" are. The aforementioned are simply displays of roaches dressed up to look like their human counterparts and displayed in a diorama depicting their circumstances. David Letteroach is likely on stage, and Liberoache at his piano. The mini-museum is the brainchild of Michael Bohdan. As the owner of the Pest Shop, a pest-control business, he comes by his subjects quite naturally.

Calling All Garden Buffs!

Clark Gardens Botanical Park is a definite must-see if you're into gardening and all things natural. The 143 acres of parkland are taken care of by the Max and Billy Clark Foundation, a not-for-profit organization that the Clarks began with a simple desire to beautify the acreage surrounding their Mineral Wells-area home. Today, a full 35-acre portion of the park is adorned with assorted varieties of trees, shrubs and blossoms, and natural pathways and water areas make up more than 50 different gardens. The park is open year-round, but hours of operation change depending on the season.

Underground Labyrinth

Texas is riddled with thousands of caves, a testament to the widely varied geology of the state. There are "wild caves" that are on private land and have only been lightly explored, and there are "show caves" that are tourist attractions. Every show cave has it's bizarre claim to fame. Longhorn Cavern, for example, was quite active as a honky-tonk during Prohibition. Maybe that's why its name rhymes with "tavern." Wonder World was formed by an earthquake and is literally a big crack in the earth. Inner Space Cavern is where scientists discovered a fossil of a saber-toothed cat.

It's Alive!

When first discovered, the Caverns of Sonora were the focus of much scientific attention. Today, visitors arrive daily to see the unique mineral formations that line several miles of cave walls. In the 1950s, the Mayfield family, who owned the ranch where the caves were found, had the roughly seven miles of caves "professionally" explored. In 1960, the caves were opened to the public, and today, visitors taking part in daily tours explore two of the seven miles. The National Natural Landmark is considered one of the most active caves in the world, with over 90 percent of the formations still growing.

Iron Horse

The Texas State Railroad State Park covers 499 acres of land between Rusk and Palestine, and not only are nature lovers drawn to the site, but folks interested in railway history are in for a great treat too. A 90-minute steam- or diesel-driven train ride in restored, historic passenger cars takes visitors from one end of the park to the other, stopping long enough for lunch before heading back. This portion of railroad was turned over to the park service in 1972, but much restoration was needed before the first tourists had a chance to ride the rails in 1976.

Women of the West

Although pioneering the wilds of this country may have been considered the accomplishment of men, one museum steadfastly heralds the contribution of the many pioneering women who labored just as tirelessly. The National Cowgirl Museum and Hall of Fame was first incarnated as the National Cowgirl Hall of Fame and Western Heritage Center in 1975. But interest in the museum was far greater than the small community of Hereford could handle. When the opportunity to move the collection to Fort Worth presented itself, all stakeholders were enthused by the prospect, and the museum doors reopened in 2002. Of the 181 women inducted into the Hall of Fame since 1975, 54 have Texas listed as their home state. They include Thena Mae Farr, co-founder of the 1947 Tri-State All Girl Rodeo; Kathryn Binford, a rancher's wife who, after her husband's death in 1934, successfully managed the family ranch while simultaneously raising two daughters and making her mark in civic politics; and Mary Ann (Molly) Goodnight who, among her numerous accomplishments, was credited with helping her husband build Goodnight College.

Looking East

There's a hint of China deep in the heart of Texas. Named after an Imperial Chinese royal community, the Forbidden City in Katy is composed of scaled down model replicas of the Terra Cotta Army, the Chinese Forbidden City complete with palace, gardens and even sculptured people, the Summer Palace, Weapons Room and Architecture Room. Altogether, the 40-acre site in Katy, which was built in 1997, tells the story of 2000 years worth of Chinese history. The project was the love child of Seattle resident Ira Poon who, wanting young people of Asian descent to know more of their history, planned and built the replica. He chose the site outside of Houston because the land was inexpensive, and because of Houston's large Asian population. One source pegs the cost of the project at about $20 million.

DID YOU KNOW?

Randall County is proud to be home to Panhandle Plains Historical Museum, the largest history museum in Texas.

SMALL TOWN ODDITIES

Ring That Bell

The town of Liberty is proud of a few things. It's the third oldest community in the state. It's rich in Spanish heritage. And in 1976, in an effort to create a symbol for the Liberty Muscular Dystrophy Foundation, and in keeping with its name, the city commissioned the White Chapel Bell Foundry in London to replicate in precise detail the original Philadelphia Liberty Bell. In the process, Liberty's Liberty Bell became the first exact replica of the original.

The Name Game

The town of Clark voted to change its name to DISH—and yes, the town's name is spelled with capital letters. The decision to rename the town after the network satellite television occurred on November 16, 2005, and it came with considerable compensation to the town's 55 homes. For 10 years, each home will receive free satellite TV, courtesy EchoStar Communications Corporation, the company's owner.

Aptly Named

If you've ever been there, it doesn't take much imagination to figure out how the Medina County farming community of Zigzag got its name. The blink-and-you-miss-it community, which once boasted a school, church, store and gin, was named for the twisting and turning road leading travelers there.

Oddly Named

The rural community of Yard received its name in a most unusual manner. Back in the early 1900s, Bruce Gray, the town's first storeowner, provided a list of possible names for the community on a bill that included a customer's order for a yard of cloth. Hence, the name Yard was officially adopted.

Iron Blessing

Folks in Blessing (population 861 based on 2000 census data), were so happy when they learned the railroad would pass through their small community, making its growth and survival a greater possibility, that ranch owner Jonathan E. Pierce thought the town should be called "Thank God." When that idea was rejected by the U.S. Postal Service, he opted for his second choice—Blessing!

DID YOU  KNOW?

Upton County has been home to two annual rattlesnake-related events since 1936—rattlesnake roundups in Rattlesnake Butte, and rattlesnake races at McCamey.

Ain't That Sweet?

The town of Poetry was originally named Turner's Point. In 1876, the U.S. Postal Service asked the community to consider changing its name because there was another similarly named community in the state. A local merchant by the name of Maston Ussery thought the area during spring reminded him of a poem, so he suggested the name Poetry.

Nothing Uncertain About It

While its name might imply instability, the 150 or so residents of Uncertain are quite sure of themselves and the value of their small community. Located on the shores of Caddo Lake, the idyllic town provides the perfect setting for human and nature to cohabit peacefully. The lake offers residents and visitors alike numerous recreation opportunities, but ironically, this is where the story of the naming of the community comes into play. The town, and initially the landing where steamboat captains would attempt to dock, got its name from its hard-to-read shoreline. It was said to be an "uncertain" shoreline, and hence, a community received its name.

Positive Karma

It's hard to imagine being grumpy when you live in a town named Happy. The community's motto is, "The town without a frown." Happy got its name in the 1890s when thirsty cowboys discovered water. They, of course, were very happy with the find.

Holubschi Heaven

Panna Maria, located near the San Antonio River and Cibolo Creek, was established on Christmas Eve in 1854 when 100 Polish immigrants arrived and celebrated their first Mass underneath an old oak tree. Although only about 41 residents still inhabit the small hamlet, based on the 2000 census, it's considered the oldest Polish settlement in the nation.

Hip Hip Hippo!

Schools with athletic teams in the small city of Hutto call themselves the Hippos—and for good reason. According to one popular legend—and there are more than a few explanations for the town's branding—in 1915, a circus hippopotamus escaped from a nearby traveling carnival and took several days vacation in a neighboring creek before it was recaptured. Concrete hippos started popping up around town, and today, when folks hear of Hutto, they immediately connect the town with its hippo history. As the school cheer goes, "You say Hutto, we say Hippo!"

Mmm-Mmm, Good!

Black's Barbecue is famous in Lockhart. Established in 1932, it has been continuously owned by the same family and is the state's oldest major barbecue restaurant. Its success obviously started somewhat of a trend, because today, the town of 11,615 people boasts four barbecue restaurants that collectively claim about 5000 patrons weekly. In 1999, the town was officially recognized as the "Barbecue Capital of Texas."

Beauty and the Book

Jefferson is home to the country's first and, so far, only beauty salon that doubles as a bookstore. In a way, the Beauty and the Book salon/store caters to the entire woman: beauty and brains. In 2000, shortly after opening up shop, owner Kathy Patrick took the notion a step further, launching the Pulpwood Queens of East Texas—a book club whose members take great pride in dressing up in the quintessential queenly manner. In fact, their motto is, "Where tiaras are mandatory and reading good books is the RULE!" To date, there are 30 chapters of Pulpwood Queens book clubs across the country.

HAUNTINGS: BELIEVE THEM OR NOT

Marfa Mystery Lights

This ghostly sight is so well documented that in 2004, a group of physics students from the University of Texas at Dallas actually traveled to the small town of just over 2100 people to study the phenomenon. The story begins back in 1883, when area resident Robert Ellison told his family stories of seeing strange, globe-like lights at night. Legend has it that he thought, perhaps, the lights belonged to Indian campfires. Others since that time also reported seeing these strange lights, and the developing oral tradition made nearby Marfa legendary.

The first official recorded report of what has come to be known as the Marfa Mystery Lights was when Paul Moran wrote "The Mystery of the Texas Ghost Light" in *Coronet* magazine in 1957. By then, there wasn't the excuse of possible campfires on a regular basis, and the lights gained a paranormal status of sorts. The 2004 research study wouldn't agree with that assessment. It concluded that most lights could be attributed to vehicle traffic. Of course, back in Ellison's day, vehicle traffic wasn't exactly a viable explanation.

Another theory credits piezoelectricity for the lights. Piezoelectricity is defined as "the ability of crystals to generate a voltage in response to applied mechanical stress." This phenomenon occurs because of the high concentration of quartz in the region. The quartz expands during the day and contracts at night, thereby creating the lights. In any case, the mysterious lights continue to draw visitors to the area, and the town has even established a Marfa Lights Festival, held every Labor Day long weekend, to celebrate the nightly wonder.

Courthouse Confessions

Paranormal practitioners and other ghost story enthusiasts in and around Corpus Christi believe the Old Nueces County Courthouse to be haunted by the spirits of criminals who met their end there. The theory has been ongoing for more than 100 years, and after one skeptic met his death in the early 1900s after reportedly being pushed out a window on the floor where death sentences were administered, it couldn't help but gain momentum. The courthouse doubled as a makeshift morgue during the 1919 hurricane, and those unsettled spirits are also thought to linger the hallways.

Black Hope Curse

This one made it on to the television show *Unsolved Mysteries*. The story goes that in 1982, a young couple that had purchased a home in the Newport subdivision in Crosby decided to add a pool to their backyard. They learned, through a stranger and later through physical evidence unearthed by the pool contractor, that their home was built on the Black Hope Cemetery—a slave cemetery. While the homeowners did everything they could to find relatives and arrange burial elsewhere, they were unsuccessful in their efforts and re-buried the unearthed coffins. The incident unleashed a series of paranormal activity, mysterious illness and even, in the case of one family member, death. Families throughout the neighborhood reported the strange phenomena, and it wasn't until the offending family moved that activity ceased.

Hauntings at the Alamo

The ghost stories of the Alamo go way back. Apparently, when Santa Anna ordered the mission destroyed, the spirits of monks who had died there years before threatened the Mexican troops. Even today, people report seeing spirits and fantastic creatures coming through the limestone walls. These reports are less surprising when you realize that the River Walk, with all kinds of fine nightclubs providing a considerable amount of alcohol, is just a block away.

1, 2, 3, Push!

The story goes that a school bus crossing a railroad in San Antonio was struck by a train, killing all the children on the bus (although the story may actually be based on a tragedy that occurred in Salt Lake City). People say that if you stop on that railroad crossing, put your car into neutral and wait, the children's spirits will push your vehicle over the tracks to safety. Many people have even put baby powder on the back of their car and claim they can see handprints all over the car. Streets in the area around the railroad crossing bear the names of children (Bobbie Allen, Cindy Sue, Laura Lee, Nancy Carole and Richey Otis). It's rumored that those are the names of children who were lost in the accident. In fact, the streets are named for the developer's grandchildren.

GHOST TOWNS

Where Did Everyone Go?

According to one website, there are almost 200 ghost towns in Texas. Most sport remnants of early settlers. Some have a few buildings still intact and safe to roam through. Others are more organized tourist locations. If you're interested in taking a trip down pioneer memory lane, there are a number of ghost town options to choose from.

Allamore

Once known as Acme, this town was located in Hudspeth County and founded in 1884 after Robert McGrew, the town's first postmaster, set up shop. By all reports it was a fledgling community from the get-go, and by 1914 the population was estimated at a scant 25. Today, all that remains are a few assorted ruins of the town's original buildings.

Bomarton

Folks interested in old churches and original pioneer schoolhouses might want to consider a trip to Bomarton. Located in Baylor County on Highway 277, the remains of the once-thriving farming community include the schoolhouse, circa 1900, a Catholic church built in the 1930s and an assortment of other buildings.

Cryer Creek

First settled in 1854, Cryer Creek grew to a population of 200 by 1892. Growth in the Navarro County community slowed shortly after that, and eventually declined until by 1990, only 15 residents were still reported living in the area. While there's not much to see of the original town site, an old grocery store still stands, and a nearby cemetery gives visitors a glimpse into the past.

Lobo

Known by some as a "modern ghost town," Lobo still boasts occupants, some of which live in the town's original buildings. The Culberson County community was founded in the 1880s, and the Southern Pacific Railroad used the town to load livestock and refill their steam engines with water. By the late 1960s, Lobo was mostly abandoned. In 1990, efforts by land developers to bring residents to the area failed, and by 1991, the town officially had a population of zero. In 2001, a group of friends decided to rebuild the ghost town into an artsy-type community, and today, 15 folks call Lobo home. They hope to renovate some of the town's original buildings, encourage all manner of artists to use the area for inspiration and host an annual music festival.

Stiles

An old courthouse is all that remains at the Stiles townsite. The Reagan County community was founded in 1894 with a post office, and actually became the Reagan County seat of justice less than a decade later. The powers that be got busy building a courthouse, which was finished in 1911, but by then the upstart town was experiencing a few glitches. The Mexico and Orient Railroad wasn't able to gain access across a piece of land and redrew their plans, taking the railroad 20 miles south of Stiles. This move, of course, meant a rival community named Big Lake was born, and Stiles suffered the setback almost immediately. The county seat moved to the new community, along with most of the residents, and all that remained was a brand new, empty courthouse.

Washington-on-the-Brazos

This town was a contender to be the capital of Texas in its early days. The Washington County community had it all—hotels, saloons, businesses, churches, schools, private homes, everything. But when Waterloo (later renamed Austin) became the capital, the railroad passed the town by. Civil War strife finished it off. All that remains today are a few street foundations and a reconstruction of Independence Hall.

BIG THINGS AND STRANGE STRUCTURES

Look Up, Look Way Up!

To say cities in Texas have some of the finest skylines in the country is an understatement. Many of the nation's tallest, most imposing buildings call Texas home. Among them, in descending order from tallest to shortest, are:

☛ P. Morgan Chase Tower, Houston: 75 stories, or 1000 feet

☛ Wells Fargo Bank Plaza, Houston: 72 stories, or 992 feet

☛ Bank of America Plaza, Dallas: 72 stories, or 921 feet

☛ Williams Tower, Houston: 64 stories, or 901 feet

☛ Renaissance Tower, Dallas: 56 stories, or 886 feet

☛ Chase Center, Dallas: 60 stories, or 787 feet

☛ Bank of America Center, Houston: 56 stories, or 780 feet

☛ Heritage Plaza, Houston: 53 stories, or 762 feet

☛ 1100 Louisianan, Houston: 55 stories, or 756 feet

☛ Towers of the Americas, San Antonio: 750 feet

Of Texas' 20 tallest buildings, 13 are located in Houston, making it the city with the country's third-tallest skyline. Six of the remaining seven are in Dallas, and one is in San Antonio.

Making a Statement

Speaking of big buildings, one of Houston's top 10 also claims bragging rights as the world's largest building located outside of a central business or main downtown area. The 64-story Williams

Tower (formerly Transco Tower), built in 1983, was designed by architects aiming for an art deco and look. Aside from its glass and steel exterior, one of the building's main features is its water wall and three-acre park, along with a beacon attached to the roof that rotates, lighting the night sky. The building took 16 months to build.

Go Figure!

With a name like Grand Saline and an economy based on salt production, it stands to reason that the community would have a salty claim to fame. The Salt Palace is the only building in North America built entirely of salt. The nearby Morton Salt Company, with salt domes 16,000 feet deep, boasts an almost endless supply of salt—enough to season the world for 20,000 years. The Salt Palace was built in 1993 and is located in the center of town.

Houston is home to Lakewood Church. The nondenominational mega church, which was founded in 1959, boasts more than 30,000 members, making it the largest church congregation in the country. To accommodate such a large group of people, the church moved to Houston's Compaq Center, which can seat 16,000 parishioners at a time.

Colossal Column

Perhaps it's because Texas is the second largest state in the country, but no one in the state ever does anything in a small way. So when organizers set out to make a memorial to remember the fallen of the Battle of San Jacinto—one of many battles on the way to Texas independence—they wanted to make a big statement. The 570-foot San Jacinto Monument, recognized as the largest of its kind in the world, makes a big statement indeed. Here are a few interesting facts on this marvel of modern architecture:

- Ground was broken for the project on April 21, 1936, though plans for the monument began immediately following the Battle of San Jacinto, 100 years earlier.

- It took 57 hours, 3800 sandwiches and 5700 cups of coffee before the 125-square-foot base of the monument was finally poured.

- The entire monument weighs more than 70 million pounds.

- It took 165 full-time workers three years to complete the project.

- The nine-pointed star gracing the top of the monument weighs 220 tons and, because of its unique configuration, can be seen as a star from any direction.

- The total cost for the project was $1.5 million, which was raised through various levels of government.

- An observation deck is located 489 feet above ground.

Nine of a Kind

The Williams Square Plaza in Irving is home to a unique tribute to the state's history. In 1976, artist Robert Glen accepted a public commission to create nine larger than life-sized mustangs for exhibit in a public mall. It took the Nairobi artist more than a year of researching the magnificent creatures, which were introduced into Texas by Spanish explorers, and the creation of numerous plasticine models before he began the finalized fiberglass and resin versions. Once complete, the mustangs were shipped to the Morris Singer Foundry in England for bronze casting before making their final journey to Irving in September 1984 and being installed at the plaza. Each of the mustangs weighs about two tons, and the sculpture is considered the world's largest equestrian sculpture.

Only in Oil Country

Back in 1928, Shell Oil decided to build a giant pit large enough to store one million barrels of crude at its Monahans site. The pit measures 426 feet across its floor and took 90 days of 24/7 manpower to complete, but in the end it was only filled with surplus oil once. It sat empty until 1987, when it and the nearby Holman House were converted into a museum and amphitheater. Visitors to the site will get a good look at Texas oil history and perhaps have a chance to take part in one of the many barbecues, chili cook-offs and other events held there.

One Long Bridge

When it was built in 1870, the 475-foot-long Waco Suspension Bridge was touted as the longest single-suspension bridge in the world by some people, and as the longest single-suspension bridge west of the Mississippi by others. Either way, after 100 years of use, the bridge was retired and is now open only to foot traffic.

A pair of 40-foot-tall cowboy boots has stood outside North Star Mall in San Antonio since 1980. The giant faux ostrich skin boots are the world's largest, and they are an icon along busy Loop 410. The immense boots were the work of Austin sculpture artist Bob "Daddy-O" Wade, who estimates that they'd hold 300,000 gallons of beer. Daddy-O (as he's known professionally) has also built other Texas icons, one being a giant saxophone in Houston made out of a surfboard, galvanized cattle troughs and recycled Volkswagen parts. He also created a football field–sized map of the United States in Dallas.

DISCOVERY

Who Discovered What?

When the Europeans showed up, 40 different Native American tribes lived in Texas, including the Apache, Cherokee and Pueblo. Several areas and cities of Texas were named after tribes in the area, including Caddo Lake, the only natural lake in Texas; Ysleta, a community outside of El Paso; and Waco and Wichita Falls, both cities.

Land Ho!

Alonso Alvarez de Pineda, outfitted with four ships and 270 men from the Spanish governor of Jamaica, was the first European to view the entire Texas coast in 1519. He mapped 800 miles of shoreline during his expedition from Florida to Veracruz. When he arrived in Veracruz, he didn't hang around. Hernan Cortes tried to capture him and he left, possibly for the Rio Grande. Or he may have settled in Jamaica. No one knows for sure.

An Eye for Trouble

During the conquest of Mexico, Panfilo de Narvaez lost both an eye and the command of his army to Hernan Cortes. Narvaez should have counted himself lucky; Cortes lay waste to the Aztec empire. Narvaez went back to Spain to lick his wounds and hit up the king for sympathy. The king apparently had a soft spot for him, because in 1528 he sent the Spaniard back to the Americas with a royal patent to establish colonies—one in Florida and one north of Veracruz. After dropping off 50 men in Florida, Narvaez loaded up the ships and headed towards Veracruz. Unfortunately, shortly after crossing the mouth of the Mississippi, the flotilla hit a violent storm. In November 1528, four survivors, including the writer Alvar Nuñez Cabeza de Vaca, were the first Europeans to set foot on Texas soil, namely Galveston Island. Cabeza de Vaca's writings became famous, describing the land in vivid detail, and his accounts stirred Spain's interest in Texas.

Claiming Texas as Home

Colonization was slow initially. Juan de Oñate, in a ceremony near present-day San Elizario in 1598, claimed the entire territory drained by the Rio Grande for Spain. Many of the initial settlements in Texas grew around missions established by the Catholic Church. The first settlement in Texas was Ysleta, established around a mission in 1682 in present day El Paso. The mission was established after the Northern New Mexico Pueblo Revolt of 1680. It's the oldest mission (by two days) in Texas.

Toast to Texas
The El Paso area, or Pass of the North, was a trade center on one of the historic *caminos reales*, or "royal highways." With the Rio Grande flowing through the area, the soil in the middle of this otherwise desert-like region was rich. Almost immediately, settlers began working with the soil. Agriculture flourished, particularly vineyards. In fact, wine and brandy made in the area were considered the best in the realm.

Texas saved the French (some would say the entire European) wine industry in 1888, when Denison resident Thomas Volney Munson developed a phylloxera-resistant grapevine. The phylloxera is a sap-sucking insect related to aphids that attacks the roots of grapevines. Since Munson used native American grape species, his work on developing them gave him the tools he needed to save French wine. And this isn't just Texas bragging—there are statues of Munson in France, and he received the French Legion of Honor. There's even a T.V. Munson Memorial Vineyard.

Planting More than Flags

People of Mexican descent in Texas trace their ancestry through the mix of Spanish men and Native women, a union that gave birth to mestizo babies starting in the 1520s. When Mexico became independent from Spain in 1821, there were as many mestizos in the area as there were Native Americans. Many of the mestizos would form the basis for the Tejanos who would fight for Texas independence.

Vive le Texas!

Robert Cavelier, Sieur de La Salle, established Fort St. Louis at Matagorda Bay in 1685, which became France's claim to Texas. But things quickly went bad for La Salle. A not-so-popular guy, La Salle was murdered by his own men two years later on his way to find the Mississippi. The remaining members of his party continued to Canada and eventually returned to France. The native Karankawas, in the meantime, killed everyone left behind at the fort a little over a year later, except for four children; they were adopted by the tribe. In a strange twist, they were rescued in 1691 and taken to Mexico to live as servants.

What's in a Nombre?

Texas was the northernmost province of Spain's North American empire. Occupied for 105 years by Spain (1716–1821), Texas was part of four provinces in the Viceroyalty of New Spain. As a result, hundreds of towns, cities, counties and geographic features of Texas have Spanish names: San Antonio (the first formal municipality in the state), Padre Island, Guadalupe Mountains, Comal, San Marcos, Pedernales River, Rio Grande, San Angelo and El Paso, to name a few.

DID YOU  KNOW?

Here's a sign of lasting influence. Of the 254 counties in the state, 42 have either a Hispanic name, an Anglicized version of a Hispanic name, such as Galveston, or a misspelling of a Hispanic name, such as Uvalde (which should have been Ugalde, after the governor of Coahuila, Mexico).

This Land is Our Land...

Mexicans claimed the Texas frontier in the early 1700s, wandering into Nacogdoches in 1716 and establishing a mission. Nothing much happened with the claim, and life continued as usual. Nacogdoches didn't become an official town until 1779, when a Spanish trader led a group there. Word traveled back and forth, and Mexico gave the settlement its first official pueblo, or town, designation.

Sun Sets on Nacogdoches

According to local history, the city of Nacogdoches is named after one of the twin sons of a Caddo chief. When the sons reached manhood, the chief sent one towards the sunrise and the other towards the sunset for three days to set up their own tribes. Nacogdoches was the name of the son who struck out towards the sunset. The other son, Natchitoches, set up camp in Louisiana.

If at First You Don't Succeed...

Nacogdoches was the site of three failed attempts to establish a Republic of Texas: the Magee-Gutierrez (1812), Long (1819) and Fredonia (1826) rebellions. Texans are nothing if not persistent.

Men with a Mission, or Five...

In 1718, five beautiful Spanish missions were located along the river in San Antonio: the Mission San Juan, which was actually moved to its present site; the Mission San Antonio de Valero, which became the Alamo; the Mission Concepcion, the best preserved; the Mission San Jose, with beautiful, colorful designs and statuary; and the Mission Espada, which started the oldest continually operating irrigation system in the U.S. Franciscan missionaries established not only these five missions, they also established every single mission in Texas. The five missions along the San Antonio River created the basis for the city's growth. Although visitors to the area in the late 1700s described it as miserable, San Antonio is now a tourist mecca.

Under New Management

The success of the Mexican War of Independence in 1821 created the Mexican Empire, which included parts of present-day Texas, New Mexico, Colorado, Arizona, California, Nevada and Utah. Land grants, which had been initiated by Spain, suddenly required considerable re-negotiation to be reauthorized with the new government.

There's nothing like practically free land to move your settlement project forward. Land grants attracted settlers from far and wide. Stephen F. Austin, who marketed the opportunity for land in New Orleans, brought 300 families to the area around the Brazos, Colorado and San Bernard rivers in 1825. Even today, families trace their ancestry to the "Old Three Hundred."

The Lone Star Button

Henry Smith, the first governor of the Mexican province of Texas, gets the credit for creating the "Lone Star" in the "Lone Star State." In 1821, Smith was just a few days into the job when he received important papers to sign. He realized, after signing them, that he didn't have an official seal. He took one of the brass buttons from his overcoat (which had a five-pointed star on it) and some sealing wax and stamped the impression of a single star on the documents. The Lone Star State was born.

TEXAS TURMOIL

History Repeats Itself

Settlers and the Mexican government just couldn't get along.
Rebellion among the Texians (as they were called then) led to
a petition for civil rights in 1833. General Antonio Lopez de
Santa Anna, who was in and out of power in Mexico, locked
up Stephen F. Austin (who delivered the petition) for two years,
charging him with treason. Then Santa Anna scrapped the
Mexican federal constitution and took up the role of dictator. That
was the last straw for the Texians. It was time to get out of Mexico.

Sam Houston: General, President, Tennessean, Cherokee Adopted Son

Sam Houston had it all going for him. He was governor of
Tennessee at age 34. In January 1829, he married 19-year-old
Eliza Allen. But something went wrong, and 11 weeks later, the
marriage ended. The breakup was tough on Houston. He
abruptly resigned from office and fled west to Indian Territory.
When he arrived in Texas, he rose to become the leader of the
unhappy settlers, who now outnumbered Mexican nationals.
Eventually, he'd become the first president of the Republic
of Texas.

DID YOU KNOW?

Sam Houston ran away from home to live with the Cherokees, possibly because he preferred not to farm or work in the family store. His Cherokee name was Colonneh, or "the Raven." When he left his governorship in 1829, he lived in self-imposed exile among the Cherokees for three years, drinking so heavily that he earned another Cherokee name: "Big Drunk." He married a Cherokee woman of mixed blood, but left her when he went to Texas.

Come and Take It!

The first shot of the Texas Revolution was fired on October 2, 1835, in Gonzales. Mexican troops demanded the return of their cannon, which they had loaned settlers. The Texans declined to give it back. Instead, they pointed it at the Mexican soldiers and said, "Come and take it." "Come and take it" became the rallying cry and the first flag of the Texas Revolution. Ten days later, the Texans took over the fort at Goliad, and within two months they took the city of San Antonio. The disputed cannon was installed at the Alamo, only to be grabbed by the Mexican army when the fort fell.

A Tough Start

The Texas Declaration of Independence was signed on March 2, 1836. Four days later, the Alamo fell to Santa Anna and his army. You could say it put a bit of a damper on the celebrations.

Remember the Alamo

No other battle is more celebrated in Texas history than the Battle of the Alamo. It has become symbolic of patriotic sacrifice in the face of overwhelming odds, not just for Texans, but for Americans as well. The Alamo itself is possibly the single most important cultural and historic site in the state, so it's a good thing the state has a few spares. Two replicas of the

Alamo exist. The first was a movie set for John Wayne's *The Alamo*, built in Brackettville (120 miles west of San Antonio) and is itself a tourist destination. The second is an exact, stone-for-stone replica of the Alamo in Houston. It is at the corporate campus of the Kwik Kopy office services chain. The building is used for company meetings.

The Siege Begins

Santa Anna, who was not particularly thrilled to have lost the northern part of his empire to the Texans, took off for San Antonio with his army of 1800. Starting on February 23, 1836, he lay siege to the Alamo, where somewhere between 189 and 257 men stood to defend the fort. When Santa Anna sent a courier to demand that the Alamo surrender, Lt. Col. William B. Travis, commander of the Alamo, replied with a cannonball.

But Travis was worried. On February 24, he wrote a letter addressed to the people of Texas and all Americans in the world. The letter later became a rallying point for the Texan army and for American support for the territory's independence. The most often quoted passage from the letter is as follows:

> *I shall never surrender or retreat. Then, I call on you in the name of Liberty, of patriotism & everything dear to the American character, to come to our aid, with all dispatch ... If this call is neglected, I am determined to sustain myself as long as possible & die like a soldier who never forgets what is due to his own honor & that of his country. Victory or Death.*
>
> *William Barret Travis*
>
> *Lt. Col. comdt*

We're Going In!

On March 5, Santa Anna stopped shelling the fort and announced to his troops an assault the next day, despite the fact that without provisions or reinforcements, it was clear surrender would be coming soon. The Mexican army of 1800 attacked at 5:00 AM on Sunday, March 6, as the Texan gunners fired. Although hundreds of Mexican troops died, the outcome was never in doubt. Travis was among the first to die; by 6:30 AM, the firing was over, and a few bloody fights took place in the long barracks. By 8:00 AM, every Alamo fighting man was dead. The Alamo had fallen.

DID YOU KNOW?

The celebrated hero of the Alamo, Lieutenant Colonel William B. Travis, didn't want to go to the fort in the first place. Although he was the chief recruiting officer for the Texan army, he'd recruited less than 10 percent of the force he thought he'd need at the remote post. "Volunteers can no longer be had or relied upon…" he wrote to the governor. Still, undermanned and out-gunned, he headed out to his post and into history.

Heroes

The heroes of the Alamo include some of Texas' most colorful figures.

- ☛ James Bowie: an adventurer known for his fiery temper and his reputation as a superb knife-fighter. He was sick with pneumonia and was killed in his bed.

- ☛ David Crockett: a Tennessee congressman who claimed to have killed a bear when he was three years old.

☞ William Barret Travis: Commander of the Alamo, he was an attorney before he became embroiled in the fight for Texas independence. He and Bowie quarreled over command; Bowie thought he should be in charge because he had brought 100 volunteers to the Alamo. They initially shared command until Bowie grew ill.

Odds and Ends About the Alamo

☞ No building can be built in San Antonio that would cause a shadow to fall on the Alamo during sunset.

☞ A very tough garrison now defends the Alamo: the Daughters of the Republic of Texas have staunchly held the shrine safe from encroaching development.

☞ According to legend, as Travis saw the hope of additional help fading, he drew a line on the ground and asked any man willing to stay and fight to step over it. All but one did.

☞ The Alamo is named for the Spanish *alamo*, meaning "cottonwood tree." A grove of cottonwoods grew right beside the fort.

On to Goliad

The Goliad Massacre is the most infamous episode in the Texas Revolution. Texan Col. James W. Fannin Jr. and his men had been captured by Mexican troops. On March 27, 1836, Santa Anna ordered the nearly 400 Texans to be executed. Unarmed and defenseless, all but 28 were killed. Those 28 managed to feign death, and three of them participated in the battle of San Jacinto.

DID YOU KNOW?

The heroine of the Texas Revolution, Francita Alavez, known as the "Angel of Goliad," was a Mexican woman who managed to enter the fort at Goliad and bring out several men, hiding them and saving their lives.

Surprise!

Santa Anna sent his troops in pursuit of General Sam Houston's forces, which had retreated to an area near Houston. After reinforcements swelled Santa Anna's troops by 500, Houston burned a bridge over Vince's Bayou. The move not only prevented more reinforcements from coming, but also cut off retreat for both armies. On April 21, during the Mexicans' afternoon siesta, the Texans moved in. Fortunately for the history of Texas, Santa Anna had not posted any lookouts. At about 3:30 in the afternoon, they charged with the cry, "Remember the Alamo! Remember Goliad!" The Battle of San Jacinto lasted 18 minutes; only nine of the 910 Texans were killed, while 630 of the Mexicans, who were caught unarmed and unorganized for battle, were killed.

DID YOU KNOW?

Sam Houston had a copy of *Gulliver's Travels* to keep him occupied before the big battle at San Jacinto.

Private Santa Anna?

Santa Anna disappeared during the battle and was found the next morning hiding in the grass, dressed as a common soldier. No one in the search party recognized him until the other prisoners referred to him as "el presidente." Later that day, nearly one million square miles of territory changed hands.

DID YOU KNOW?

The Mexican general, Santa Anna, was terrified of water and could barely bring himself to cross a river.

The Twin Sisters: Texas' Most Famous Pair of Cannons

A belated thank you to Ohio! The citizens of Cincinnati donated two smoothbore cannons to help the Texas Revolution.

The cannons were intended to help out with the Alamo. Unfortunately, that fight was over too soon. When they reached the Texas army on April 11, 1836, however, they were just in time for the next big fight, the Battle of San Jacinto. They could fire at a distance of 200 yards, and it's believed that they were critical to the success of the attack. The Mexican army, which was used to a more organized approach to battle, was thrown into confusion, and the chaos helped the Texan infantry swarm the lines. You wouldn't have found many cannonballs on the battlefield, though. Because the Texas army had no ammo, the Twins fired musket balls, broken glass and horseshoes.

We Left Them Here, Somewhere...

When Texas joined the United States, the Twins were turned in as a condition of joining the union. They were rolled out again briefly during the Civil War. Once Texas, which was on the Confederate side, lost, the state was again required to turn in all armaments. This, of course, included the Twins. Yet somehow, the two cannons "disappeared." Some people believe a group of Confederates buried them somewhere in Houston and failed to tell anyone exactly where.

The Yellow Rose of Texas

The legend goes that Emily D. West, an African-American woman, seduced Santa Anna, allowing him to be distracted when the Texans attacked in the battle of San Jacinto. The reality is probably a little different, and much less romantic. Historians believe that if West was with Santa Anna, it was not by choice, nor is it likely she played any part in the battle. West was a free African-American orphan who migrated to Texas in 1835. She became known as Emily Morgan because she was a servant of James Morgan, a Texas plantation owner. Santa Anna captured her when he invaded the area prior to the Battle of San Jacinto. Her beauty and the legend are said to have inspired the song "The Yellow Rose of Texas." The Emily Morgan Hotel in San Antonio is named after her as well.

Independence Streak Comes to a Halt at the Bank

The Texas Declaration of Independence, enacted on March 2, 1836, had been enforced. By April, the Texans had battled their way to freedom. The Republic of Texas was ready for business. And then the bills arrived. Texas was recognized as a republic by the U.S., France, the UK, the Netherlands and the Republic of Yucatan. But the fight for independence had been darn expensive, hostilities with Mexico seemed unending and, as the creditors came knocking at the door, independence seemed less and less appealing. The U.S. agreed to defend the coast *and* pay the bills if the republic signed up for statehood, and so nine years, 11 months and 17 days after its declaration of independence, Texas became a state.

This Land is My Land

Still, they were tough negotiators in Texas. As a condition of annexation, the state did not have to surrender its public lands to the federal government like virtually every other state. Texas did grant all territory outside of its current area to the federal government in 1850, but it did not cede any public lands within its boundaries at the time. Essentially, the only Texas lands owned by the federal government had to be purchased by the government.

Here We Go Again

Governor Sam Houston tried to avoid the demands for a convention to decide which side Texas should be on in the Civil War. After working so hard to get Texas to be part of the Union, he wasn't too thrilled to see it all go down the musket barrel, so to speak. Stalling didn't work. Although only one in four Texas families owned slaves, the state voted to side with the Confederate States of America in 1861. By the end of that year, there were 25,000 Texans in the Confederate army, most in the cavalry. It's estimated that 90,000 Texans were in military service during the Civil War. A string of Confederate military defeats began to mount up, and Robert E. Lee surrendered in April 1865. Unsurprisingly perhaps, Texans continued to fight.

The last battle of the Civil War was in Texas—the Battle of Palmito Ranch (near Brownsville) on May 13, 1865. Even though the Texas Confederates won the battle, the war was clearly already over. When soldiers learned from some of their captured prisoners that the Confederate forces were surrendering everywhere else, they headed for home.

Some People Just Can't Accept Change

The Republic of Texas resurfaced briefly in 1997, when Richard McLaren kidnapped his neighbors in the Davis Mountains, 175 miles southeast of El Paso. Calling himself the ambassador and chief legal counsel for the sovereign Republic of Texas, McLaren had been issuing liens against property, trillions of dollars in judgments against U.S. and state agencies and even license plates. The Republic of Texas group believed Texas was illegally annexed into the United States.

Things heated up considerably when "Ambassador" McLaren, along with his fellow Republic of Texas members, held Margaret Ann Rowe and her husband, Joe Rowe, captive in retaliation for the arrest of two Republic of Texas members in 1997. He also ordered his militia members to begin picking up federal judges, legislators and IRS agents for immediate deportation. Nearly 300 state troopers and Texas Rangers showed up at the neighborhood and laid siege for a week to McLaren and his supporters' "embassy" until the kidnappers agreed to lay down their weapons. McLaren was sentenced to 99 years for the kidnapping and standoff and an additional 12 years for 26 counts of mail and bank fraud and conspiracy. McLaren's "embassy" was later purchased by a nature conservation group that manages an adjacent land preserve.

CITIES AND THEIR TRIVIA

A Capital Idea

Forty-seven different communities in Texas have laid claim to one accomplishment or another. That could be why Texas is considered the "World Capital of Capitals." For some communities, it's about the crops they grow. For others, it's something they do well. Either way, the list of special designations is quite extensive, and believe it or not, these are all official.

Place Name	Claim to Fame	When Designated
Anahuac	Alligator Capital of Texas	1989
Baird	Antique Capital of Texas	1993
Breckenridge	Mural Capital of Texas	2001
Brownsville	Chess Capital of Texas	2003
Burnet County	Bluebonnet Co-capital of Texas	1981
Caldwell	Kolache Capital of Texas	1989

(A *kolache* is a Czech bread pastry with fruit or meat filling)

Place Name	Claim to Fame	When Designated
Clifton	Norwegian Capital of Texas	1997
Comal County	Volunteer Capital of Texas	1997
Commerce	Bois d'Arc Capital of Texas	1999

(A *bois d'arc*, for folks who don't hail from Commerce, is a small tree also called the Osage-orange. It is known for its spherical, bumpy fruit, which is filled with sticky, white sap.)

Place Name	Claim to Fame	When Designated
Danevang	Danish Capital of Texas	1999
Denison	White Root Stock Capital of the World	1989
DeWitt County	Wildflower Capital of Texas	1999
Electra	Pump Jack Capital of Texas	2001
Elgin	Sausage Capital of Texas	1995
Ennis	Bluebonnet City of Wetaskiwin	1997
Fredericksburg	Polka Capital of Texas	1993
Gatesville	Spur Capital of Texas	2001
George West	Storyfest Capital of Texas	1995
Georgetown	Red Poppy Capital of Texas	1990
Glen Rose	Dinosaur Capital of Texas	1997
Hawkins	Pancake Capital of Texas	1995
Hearne	Sunflower Capital of Texas	1997

Hutto	Hippo Capital of Texas	2003
Jefferson	Bed and Breakfast Capital of Texas	1997
Kenedy	Texas Horned Lizard Capital of Texas	2001
Knox City	Seedless Watermelon Capital of Texas	1997
Lamar County	Crape Myrtle County Capital	1997
Llano County	Bluebonnet Co-capital of Texas	1981
Lockhart	Barbecue Capital of Texas	1999
Longview	Purple Martin Capital of Texas	1991
Mauriceville	Crawfish Capital of Texas	1983
McCamey	Wind Energy Capital of Texas	2001
Mesquite	Rodeo Capital of Texas	1993
Midland	Ostrich Capital of Texas	1991
Odessa	Jackrabbit-Roping Capital of Texas	2001
Paris	Crape Myrtle City	1997
Parker County	Peach Capital of Texas	1991
Plano	Hot Air Balloon Capital of Texas	1999
Rains County	Eagle Capital of Texas	1995
Round Rock	Daffodil Capital of Texas	2003
Sanderson	Cactus Capital of Texas	1999
Temple	Wildflower Capital of Texas	1991
Waxahachie	Crape Myrtle Capital of Texas	1997
Weslaco	Citrus Capital of Texas	1997
West	Czech Heritage Capital of Texas	1997
West	Kolache Home of Texas Legislature	1997
West Tawakoni	Catfish Capital of Texas	2001
Wills Point	Bluebird Capital of Texas	1995

EL PASO

In 1940, the El Paso Electric Company built a 50-foot-wide star on the leading edge of the mountain that comes through the center of the city. Originally built as the city's biggest holiday decoration, the 50-foot star was quickly considered too small—it couldn't be seen from one of the nearby highways, and many of the bulbs were blown out by a storm. Improvements were made in 1940, and the star was increased to 459 feet long by 278 feet wide. The dimensions are altered in this way because the star sits on the mountain at a 30° angle, so it appears perfect from the city below. It's visible from 100 miles in the air and 30 miles on the ground. It takes 459 150-watt bulbs to light the star. The star remained lit for the first time beyond the holiday season in 1979 in recognition of the American hostages held in Iran. Then the star was lit again and remained lit for eight months during the Persian Gulf War in 1990–91. In 1993, local officials spearheaded a movement to keep the star lit throughout the year, and as of April 21, 1993, the star became a nightly feature on the mountain.

Crikey! Is That an Alligator? In the Desert?

There are many stories as to how alligators came to be a central attraction in El Paso's San Jacinto Plaza. Some people claim they were sent to a local miner as a joke from a friend in Louisiana. Others claim that the El Paso Parks and Streets Commissioner brought them in a box and kept them in a barrel of water at a local saloon until the pond was built in the plaza. However they got there, the alligators became a central attraction in 1883, and in time there were seven of them. The alligators have had their share of adventure. One was relocated to a college professor's office; another was set loose in a swimming pool at the college right before an intramural swim meet. One

was the object of a "guess my weight contest," with the prize being $100 and a trip to Mexico. Eventually, the alligators had to be removed and relocated to the El Paso zoo because of acts of vandalism and cruelty.

Now I Feel Safe
The El Paso City Council once voted to spend over $100,000 for private security to guard the city police station.

DID YOU  KNOW?

El Paso is known as the "Sun City." The sun shines in El Paso 302 days per year on average.

Click Your Heels
El Paso has a unique claim to fame when it comes to heralding itself as a Texas capital. With a plethora of boot companies calling the city home, it eventually designated itself as the state's "Boot-making Capital." Tony Lama was the town's first boot maker, setting up shop back in 1911.

The city is home to the 24,000-acre Franklin Mountains State Park, the largest urban park in the U.S. The Franklin Mountains are the largest sustained mountain range in the state, and the summit of North Franklin Peak rises 3000 feet above the city. The park has 118 miles of hiking trails, 51 miles of which are also available for mountain biking and 22 miles of which are open for horseback riding. The Trans-Mountain road cuts through the mountain, linking the west and east side of the city. The park is home to golden eagles, hawks and falcons, all of which claim this northern part of the Chihuahuan Desert as home.

Military Moves

El Paso's biggest boom in population came in the 1910s, when the town's population grew by 60,000 people all trying to escape the bloody Mexican Revolution. Another similar boom is expected in 2007, when 50,000 people are slated to move to the area because of expansion of the local military base, Fort Bliss. The fort is the second largest military installation next to White Sands Missile Range (right up the road in New Mexico) in the U.S. Army. With 1.1 million acres, Fort Bliss' mission is air defense artillery, particularly the maintenance of several Patriot Missile batteries. The base is being realigned to be a heavy armor training post, and by 2011, the number of troops will rise from roughly 7000 to 23,000—making El Paso the only area in the U.S. to have a major gain in forces.

HOUSTON

Have Plastic, Will Shop…and Shop…and Shop!
Texas' largest shopping mall is the Galleria in Houston. It sits at one of the busiest road intersections in the country and consists of three office towers, two hotels and a private health club. The idea of combining an indoor mall with a hotel came from oilman Glenn H. McCarthy in the 1950s, but it never went past the idea phase. Nearly 20 years later, the concept was developed by Gerald D. Hines in 1970. It started out with 600,000 square feet of retail space, skylights and three hanging chandeliers. By 2006, retail space was up to 2.4 million square feet, and the mall now includes a full sized ice rink under a glass atrium. Over 24 million visitors come to the Galleria every year.

So That's Why There Are So Many Mosquitoes

Once upon a time, Houston was a swamp. Soggy and sodden in the junction of the Buffalo and White Oak bayous, it certainly seemed an unlikely location for the fourth-largest city in the U.S. Yet, something about the bayou inspired settlement. Very little of the original swamp land remains in the city (until there's a flood—more on that later). In fact, the Armand Bayou Nature Center is about all that's left intact. The nature center is a 2500-acre preserve of a wetland in the center of the highly urbanized area between NASA/Johnson Space Center and the Bayport Industrial District. It is one of four Texas Coastal Preserves, and it is the last bayou in Houston that has not been channeled. It's not only a wetland, it also has bottomland forest and tall grass prairie—all of which used to exist in the area before people started draining the swamp, moving the alligators and building skyscrapers.

It's Noon and 100 Degrees in Houston— Where Is Everybody?

If you're looking for the population of downtown Houston at noon during the week, you'll have to look underground. Open only during weekdays from 6:00 AM to 6:00 PM, the city has a six-mile system of tunnels that link 95 city blocks in subterranean and, most importantly considering the sweltering heat of Houston, climate-controlled pedestrian walkways. Combined with aboveground skywalks, most buildings downtown—hotels, banks, offices, restaurants, retail stores and the Theater District—are all connected through the system. The tunnel system started in the 1930s as a connection between two downtown movie theaters. The current system took shape during Houston's construction boom of the 1960s and 1970s. There are some areas not connected to the main system, notably the county courts, jails and other related buildings.

Plugging the Drain

All of Houston's Harris County is made up of bayous and ditches to carry rainwater to the Gulf of Mexico. As the city has grown and replaced dirt with concrete, it's lost its prairie and the vast sponge of swamp land. Yet the cycle of torrential rains that fed the swamps for years still exists, skyscrapers or no skyscrapers. In any rain, the natural runoff into the bayous increases both in quantity and speed. Add to that a little weather pattern called a hurricane, and you have the formula for a flood. In the past 35 years, there have been eight 100-year floods and three 500-year floods. During these floods, large sections of the interstate and many neighborhoods have ended up under water. Tropical Storm Allison caused the worst flood damage in recent Texas history when it blew through in 2001. The stormed poured over two feet of water onto Houston in June. It destroyed highways, drove 17,000 people to shelters and caused $5 billion in damage. Some 70,000 homes were affected.

DID YOU KNOW?

The terms "100-year flood" and "500-year flood" are a little misleading. They don't mean that these floods come around once every 100 or 500 years, they mean that the percentage chance of them coming in any given year is one percent for the 100-year flood or 0.2 percent for the 500-year flood.

DALLAS

Naming Rights

So why is it called Dallas? No one is quite sure, although theories abound. It may be named after George Mifflin Dallas, who was the 11th U.S. vice president back in the days of the city's founding. However, the founder of the city, John Neely Bryan, never mentioned having met the VP, and the city was founded before George Mifflin Dallas became VP. There was also the vice president's brother, Commodore Alexander J. Dallas of the U.S. Navy, but again, no connection has ever been made between Bryan and the commodore. Possibly Joseph Dallas, just a regular guy who had settled nearby in 1843, was the inspiration. Then there were James and Walter Dallas. James was a Texas Ranger and Walter fought at San Jacinto.

Stop the Presses!

The first newspaper printed in Dallas hit the streets in 1849 and was known as the *Cedar Snag*. Up until the 1990s, Dallas, like many American cities, had two newspapers. Now, the *Dallas Morning News* runs one of the largest newspaper printing facilities in the country, with eight presses sitting on 29 acres in nearby Plano. With a circulation of nearly 650,000, it needs every single one of those presses. The *Dallas Morning News* has won eight Pulitzer Prizes.

The Ebb and Flow in Deep Ellum

Deep Ellum, just east of downtown Dallas, was the center for music and art in the city. In 1937, a newspaper columnist described it as the "one spot in the city that needs no daylight saving time because there is no bedtime." The name Deep Ellum is a blurring of the phrase "deep Elm Street." The arts and entertainment district was a center for jazz and blues in the 1920s and '30s, and had another renaissance in the 1960s and

'70s when artists took over cheap warehouse spaces. In the 1980s, Deep Ellum became even more colorful when graffiti artists took over. The city allowed local artists to paint the walls of the Good-Latimer Tunnel, which is a primary entrance to the neighborhood. The artists adopted a graffiti style, and over time, music venues began to use graffiti to advertise upcoming shows. There is so much graffiti in Deep Ellum that many people believe that it's legal (it's not). Deep Ellum has lately been in a recession of sorts, because of an increase in crime.

TEXAS SIZED

Dallas is home to a 67.5-foot-tall bronze giraffe that looks over Interstate Highway 35 East. It is the tallest statue in the state—15 feet taller than Big Tex—and is built to withstand 100-mile-per-hour winds (given that Dallas is in Tornado Alley, this seems to be a reasonable precaution). The giraffe stands in front of the zoo and has its tongue sticking out and up into the air, presumably looking for a 70-foot-tall tree.

The Depository and the President

One of the most infamous incidents in Dallas history took place on November 22, 1963, when President John F. Kennedy was assassinated. The president's motorcade was making its way through Dealey Plaza, just a few yards away from the spot John Neely Bryan had first settled in 1841. Riding with the president was his wife, Governor John B. Connally and Connally's wife. As the car started down Elm Street, several shots where fired and both Kennedy and Connally were hit. The president was pronounced dead from wounds in the neck and head. The governor recovered from wounds in his back, wrist and thigh. Lee Harvey Oswald was arrested in the Texas Theatre, but he was not initially charged with the assassination; he was charged with the murder of a policeman, J.D. Tippit. The next day, Oswald was charged with the assassination, and the day after that he was killed in front of television cameras by a Dallas nightclub owner, Jack Ruby. Every year, over two million visitors come to Dealey Plaza to visit the site of the assassination. In 1989, the city established a museum, the Sixth Floor Museum, with a permanent historical exhibition on John F. Kennedy. It's called the Sixth Floor because the sixth floor of the school book depository (and the site of the museum) is where a sniper's nest and rifle were found.

AUSTIN

Going Batty!

Austin is nicknamed Silicon Hills in recognition of the count-less technological corporations that call that city home, applauded as the Live Music Capital of the World…and well known for its abundance of Mexican free-tailed bats. The bats converged on the city after repairs and renovations were made to the Congress Avenue Bridge in 1980. It was a feat of engineer-ing magnificence, but the powers-that-be involved in the project didn't know a whole lot about bats and, inadvertently, provided the loveable nocturnal creatures with a perfect nesting area in the abundance of crevices under the bridge.

Although it admittedly took a little while for residents to get used to the 1.5 million bats emerging into the night sky throughout the summer months, the city has come to appreciate the many benefits of the experience: Austin is now known as the habitat for the largest urban bat colony in the world; as many as 100,000 people line the bridge at night to witness the natural wonder; 10,000 to 20,000 pounds of mosquitoes and other pests are consumed by the bats nightly; and the whole natural phenomenon brings in about $10 million in tourist revenue each year. I'd say the bridge, and the bats, have pretty much paid for themselves.

If you have a wide silicone rubber band around your wrist denoting support for diabetes, your local school or a rock bank, you can thank the Austin-based Lance Armstrong Foundation, which was started with a focus on increasing both research and awareness of testicular cancer, but now works to inspire and empower people with all forms of cancer. The bright yellow wristbands (yellow was chosen because it's the color of the jersey worn by the lead cyclists in the Tour de France) were originally part of a campaign to raise $5 million for the Foundation in cooperation with Nike (who manufactured and sold the wristbands in their stores). Little did the folks at the Foundation know what they would unleash on the world. Their fundraising target was surpassed in six months, and as of 2007, there have been more than 70 million "Livestrong" bands sold. It didn't take long for other organizations to adopt the idea for their own fundraising, including pink bands for breast cancer, red for heart disease and camouflage for veterans wounded in battle.

SAN ANTONIO

Chill Out!

The Milam Building in San Antonio was the first fully air-conditioned high rise in the U.S. Built in 1928, the 21-story building used pipes to carry chilled water past fans that circulated the air.

Bring Out the Puppets!

After a flood in 1921 put nine feet of water onto Houston Street and killed 50 people, the people of San Antonio demanded flood control. The original plan was to turn the existing riverbed (where the River Walk now is) into a sewer. The local Conservation Society almost had a heart attack. They put on a puppet show at City Hall and took the commissioners on canoe rides to show them the river in an attempt to convince them it was worth saving. It worked, and the River Walk is now the city's most visited attraction.

GRAPE AND GRAIN

Drink Up! No, Not There! Over Here!

Texas has 42 dry counties, which means these are counties where it is illegal to sell alcohol. But we're talking about Texas law, so the rules can be confusing. There are 169 partially "moist" counties, where you can get an alcoholic beverage by jumping through a few hoops. For example, you may have to join a "club," which usually entails signing a card with your server, before you're allowed to buy liquor by the drink. In some semi-dry counties, you can buy beer but not wine or liquor. In Grand Prairie, you can't find beer, but you can buy liquor at area restaurants. In Plano, a Hooters restaurant had to move its front door so it wouldn't be considered too close to a church to sell alcohol. There's a strip of huge package liquor stores with giant neon signs just outside the Lubbock County line, and it is regularly jammed with customers. The complex maze of laws is probably a holdover from Prohibition. In fact, until 1972, you couldn't legally buy a mixed drink in Texas.

Brewed in Texas

The oldest independent brewery in Texas is in Shiner. Founded in 1909, the Spoetzl Brewery is best known for it's dark Czech-style beer, Shiner Bock. One of its longest brewmasters was immigrant Kosmos Spoetzl. Kosmos worked for eight years at the Pyramids Brewery in Cairo, moved to Canada and then moved to San Antonio in search of better weather. He and a partner leased the brewery in 1915. Then came Prohibition. Spoetzl survived by selling ice and near beer. When the big breweries came back after Prohibition ended, life got tough for independent breweries. But Spoetzl kept things small and simple. He never went more than 70 miles for business, and by 1990, production was only at 36,000 barrels. Then the word must have spread, because by 2004, production was up to 300,000 barrels.

 Since Shiner Bock is a dark beer, the creation of Shiner Light was a big deal. It went through a taste-testing ballot by the residents of Shiner and is only available in Texas. Every label of Shiner Light bears the signature of a Shiner resident.

A Well-Traveled Beer

Lone Star is one of the state's best-known brews. In 1959, the brewery in San Antonio had a reputation as the world's most beautiful brewery. The Lone Star name and formula were bought by Pabst Brewing in 1999, with production eventually moving into the Pearl Brewery in San Antonio. The Pearl Brewery was then deemed too old (it had been built around the turn of the century) to be modernized, and in 2001, Lone Star moved north. It's now produced in Fort Worth in a Miller brewery.

Pearl was the only brewery in San Antonio to have survived Prohibition, thanks to Emma Koehler. After years of producing near beer and bottling soft drinks, Koehler was ready for the end of Prohibition. She restarted beer production only 15 minutes after Prohibition ended in Texas on September 15, 1933.

DID YOU  KNOW?

The San Antonio Museum of Art, known for it's Mexican folk art and pre-Columbian and Spanish Colonial collections, is housed in what was once the Lone Star Brewery.

Sunday Wine

Winemaking started in Texas practically the day the missionaries arrived—for sacramental purposes, of course. The first vineyard of black Spanish grapes was planted in 1662 at the Ysleta Mission near El Paso, and wine produced there was considered the finest in the land. Now there are 3500 acres "under vine" in Texas, and the state is the fifth largest producer of wine in the U.S. Wine production in 2005 was estimated at 1.5 million gallons, and there are 113 wineries in the state. The largest winery in Texas is Llano Estacado in the Panhandle, with an annual production of 120,000 cases. Llano's 1986 Chardonnay won double gold at a San Francisco Fair wine competition, and since then Texas wines have continued winning medals at national and international competitions. Most of the wine is Cabernet Sauvignon, with Chardonnay filling glasses at the other end of the bar.

Wine at its Finest

Attention wine lovers everywhere. You may want to check out a bottle of wine from the Val Verde Winery in Del Rio. Founded in 1883 by Italian immigrant Frank Qualia, the family-run business claims to be the oldest continuously running winery in Texas. Even Prohibition couldn't shut it down; it just produced wine for "medicinal purposes" during that time. Today, more than 120 years after it first opened for business, Val Verde Winery remains in the Qualia family. And with that much experience, it can't help but be one of the best!

GAMES PEOPLE PLAY

Scratch Here

Since Ann Richards bought the first ticket in 1992, the Texas Lottery has generated $14 billion for the state. Since 1997, all Texas Lottery proceeds have been transferred to the Foundation School Fund for public education.

DID YOU KNOW?

Gambling in Texas is illegal, except for the lottery, charitable bingo and animals running in circles.

B-7? Bingo!

Charitable bingo attracts millions of players. In 2006, over 19 million people played in venues ranging from church and VFW halls to bingo parlors. The games are complex, with a wide range of variations. Some games involve marking only the corners, some require getting all the numbers along the edges, and there's always the usual straight line. Closely supervised by the state, proceeds from bingo are designated for charity only. Texas charities received $31.7 million in 2006 alone, and players won $489 million.

Wanna Bet? Hop in the Car

With the Kickapoo tribe only running bingo and poker games at the Lucky Eagle along the border, what's a one-armed bandit fan to do? Hit the road. Most of the casino gambling by Texans happens in Louisiana, Oklahoma and New Mexico. In fact, the vast majority of license plates in the out-of-state casino parking lots proudly display the Texas flag. Gambling interest groups have taken their case to the Legislature for decades, but historically, gambling tends to occupy the same spot on the state's political map as a state income tax—a Texas no-no.

Get the Bunny!

Most of the real gambling in Texas takes place in one of two places—on the reservation or at the track. There are three greyhound race tracks, and 19 greyhound rescue groups, in Texas.

In the 1930s, there was a traveling group of jockeys on greyhounds—monkeys. There was considerable monkey business during races, though. There are tales of these miniature jockeys pulling at the pseudo-saddles on competitors during a race, which made for a tough job for odds makers. Racing greyhounds are retired after a few short years of chasing the bunny around the track.

I Like My Racing a Wee Bit Taller…

If horses are more your speed, you can find them making the run at four race tracks across the state. Horse racing, the first organized Anglo-Texan sport, got going after the Texas Revolution. There was an active racing circuit along the Gulf Coast. Then betting was outlawed in 1937. Sure, Texans could still race, but somehow, racing in a circle just for the thrill of it never caught on. Go figure. Fifty years later in 1987, pari-mutuel wagering was legalized, and Texas got back into the dirt. Manor Downs, in Austin, is the oldest pari-mutuel track in Texas, but the first Class 1 racetrack opened in 1994 in northwest Houston, the Sam Houston Race Park. Retama Park was hot on its heels, or hooves, in 1995. Lone Star Park in Grand Prairie is the fourth track.

Famous Texas Horses

☞ Assault, a horse from Texas's most famous ranch, the King Ranch, won the Triple Crown in 1946. When Assault was retired to stud, tests showed him to be sterile. But when turned out with eight mares, he fathered four foals. Apparently he just needed a little sweet-talking.

☞ San Antonio's Cass Ole', one of the most honored Arabian show horses in the country, was the star of *The Black Stallion*. Highly intelligent and beautiful, Cass Ole' was not completely black; the star on his forehead and patches on his legs were white and had to be dyed for the film. His statue still stands above the gate to the San Antonio Arabians Ranch, which has recently been converted to include a rodeo arena.

☞ Shiloh, though not from Texas, is given credit for establishing many great Texan quarter horse bloodlines. Like Sam Houston, Shiloh was from Tennessee.

DID YOU  KNOW?

Arlington Downs opened in 1929, when wagering on the ponies was still illegal. Oil and cattle magnate William T. Waggoner placed a $3 million bet that it would become legal in due time. In the meantime, two men were arrested at Arlington Downs in 1931 for opening betting on races. The resulting publicity got the attention of the Texas Legislature, and two years later, all bets were on. Then all bets were off again in 1937 when the laws were repealed.

THE OLDEST PROFESSION

Red Lights

Prostitution set up shop in various cities across the state in the late 1800s with some very colorful names. Dallas had Frogtown and Boggy Bayou and Houston had Happy Hollow. Fort Worth called its vice district Hell's Half-Acre, and San Antonio kept it simple with the District. But no city had a vice district as famous as La Grange's Chicken Ranch.

The Chicken Ranch

Until 1973, the Chicken Ranch may have been the oldest continuously running brothel in the U.S. In 1844, Mrs. Swine set up shop in a small hotel with three young women from New Orleans. During the Civil War, Swine and Tillie, a prostitute, were run out of town, accused of being Yankees. Jessie Williams took over, moving the operation to two houses on 11 acres just outside the city limits, and the brothel continued its services. In 1917, Williams promoted two sisters to "middle management," putting them in charge of public relations. They sent packages and letters to local boys fighting in World War I. When the Depression hit, customers didn't have cash, so they paid in chickens. Soon there were chickens everywhere, and Williams had a side business in eggs and poultry.

Edna Milton took over the Chicken Ranch in the 1950s and became one of La Grange's biggest philanthropists. It was estimated that the Chicken Ranch had an income of more than $500,000 a year. Milton ran the ranch successfully until 1973, when a TV expose forced state officials to shut it down—despite significant protests by the local community. A musical about the ranch, *The Best Little Whorehouse in Texas*, was a hit in 1978 and was made into a movie in 1982 starring Dolly Parton.

LET THE GOOD TIMES ROLL!

Party!

Texas knows how to party and has some of the most interesting festivals and nightspots dedicated to good times.

Out with a Flash

The city of Galveston, originally known as Campeche, found itself in rebuilding mode very early in its history. Infamous pirate Jean Lafitte set up shop in the village back in 1817. Four years later, Lafitte was asked to leave after attacking an American ship. Of course, he wasn't going out with a whimper. Before he left town, he hosted a once-in-a-lifetime party that ended only after Campeche had burned to the ground.

The Biggest Party in Texas...or Anywhere

Fiesta San Antonio is a 10-day, city-wide celebration with over 150 events. It's been called the largest public festival in the country, with 75,000 volunteers, 3.5 million attendees and an economic impact of $250 million. It started out as a parade to honor the heroes of the Alamo and San Jacinto, and the parades have maintained the spotlight even with the addition of 150 events, including a spoof on local politics, a celebration of oysters, a jazz festival and a croquet tournament, to name a few. Fiesta kicks off every year in April with King Antonio, the king of Fiesta, snipping off the tie of the mayor of San Antonio.

☞ The Battle of Flowers Parade started with the tossing of flowers by the Daughters of the Alamo in a symbolic battle in front of the Alamo. Now it's the reason schools and businesses close for half the day. The parade is produced entirely by women.

☞ The Texas Cavaliers River Parade winds around the San Antonio River Walk. One year, the small barge featuring Ray Feo (the people's king) began to sink, and the band on board jumped ship. With their collective weight gone, the barge rose again and continued down the river.

☞ The Flambeau Night Parade attracts half a million people and features more than 50 floats, 40 bands and Fiesta royalty. It's America's largest illuminated night parade.

How Fiesta Is Different from Mardi Gras

At all the parades during Fiesta, people along the side of the route yell to the women on the floats, "Show us your shoes!" And, as is tradition, the women, who are decked from head to toe in glittering gowns and headdresses, lift their royal skirts and flash their shoes at the crowd. Given the length of the parade and the weight of the royal gowns, it's no surprise when the shoes are not the usual high heels—most often the styles range from flip flops to jeweled sneakers to decked out house slippers.

Whatever the event in Fiesta, the cascarone is the one constant symbol you'll find everywhere. Over 100,000 empty eggshells are colored and stuffed with confetti for Fiesta. Then the fun begins. No setting is too sacred to have your head bashed with a cascarone during Fiesta. In fact, it's considered good luck to be struck with one. Although historians have traced cascarones back to Renaissance Italy, their use in mass frivolity was definitely born in San Antonio.

A Texas-Sized Fair

The State Fair of Texas has taken place in Dallas since 1886. Proclaimed the largest state fair in the U.S., over three million people visit the fair over 24 days in the fall. It features some of the most unusual deep-fried foods of any fair. Deep-fried Oreo cookies, deep-fried Twinkies and deep-fried peanut butter, jelly and banana sandwiches are all available to brave souls with little care about their cholesterol levels.

Big Tex looms over the crowd at the State Fair. With his 75-gallon hat, and standing 52 feet tall in his boots, Big Tex is the world's tallest talking cowboy. Yes, Big Tex talks, thanks to sound engineers in 1953. He's a little slow, but understandable—sort of like a cowboy at closing time. He started waving in 1997, and by the year 2000, he could turn his head to see what was going on all around him. In 2002, he turned 50 and got both a giant cake and an AARP card.

There are some little known facts about Big Tex. His clothes are actual clothes, made of cloth, and the pants alone weigh 80 pounds. And Tex wasn't always a cowboy. He started out with a stint as Santa in 1949 for the Kerens Chamber of

Commerce. Thanks to Dallas artist and stage designer Jack
Bridges, Big Tex found a second career when he left Kerens to
seek other opportunities. Bridges managed to transform Big Tex
from his North Pole self into the ultimate cowboy.

The fair features the largest Ferris wheel in
North America, the Texas Star. It rises 212 feet
and can give 260 people a go-round. There are
16,000 turbolights and 880 lights on the
44 gondolas.

Tragedy at the Fair

In 1955, three high school band girls fell from a different Ferris wheel at the State Fair, the Sky Wheel. The school band had performed in the Cotton Bowl and, during a break, the girls decided to go for a ride on the Ferris wheel. At the top of the wheel, the seat broke and all three girls fell from a height of 92 feet. Two of the girls survived, while the third died from injuries sustained in the fall.

When Pooh Parties

You'd think Eeyore's Birthday Party in Austin would be a fairly glum affair, or something designed for the five-and-under set. You would be wildly wrong. Eeyore's Birthday Party is a day-long festival featuring huge drum circles, colorful costumes and significant use of recreational drugs. It's the type of event that appeals to Austin's modern-day hippies, with an attendance in the thousands. A statue that combines the Statue of Liberty with Eeyore, called the Eeyore of Liberty, frequently stands over the dance circle.

That's a Whole Lot of Beer

Billy Bob's Texas promotes itself as the "world's largest honky-tonk," and if it isn't the biggest, it's darn close. The building, built in Fort Worth in 1910, has grown into a 127,000-square-foot nightclub with several dance floors, stages, arcade games and a small indoor rodeo arena for weekend bull riding. Back in 1910, the site of Billy Bob's was a large, open-air barn where prize cattle hung out and chewed the cud during sets at the Fort Worth Stock Show. Then, as part of a Texas Centennial Project in 1936, the city enclosed the barn and added a tower. That's also when the auction ring was added, which became the bull-riding arena.

Billy Bob's opened as an actual nightclub in 1981. There are three acres of space inside, 20 acres of parking and 32 bar stations.

It has an over 6000-person capacity and can serve up a good bit of beer. The most beer sold in one night was at a Hank Williams Jr. concert—a total of 16,000 bottles. The bar is often compared to Gilley's in Houston, which was featured in *Urban Cowboy*. Gilley's, by comparison, is 44,000 square feet and has only mechanical bulls, not live pro bulls, as Billy Bob's is quick to point out.

Where Is It? The Sign Is Missing!
The saying goes that everybody is somebody in Luckenbach. Founded in 1849, Luckenbach has grown to legendary status, thanks to two Texas legends: Jerry Jeff Walker, who recorded a live album in the dance hall there, and Willie Nelson, who recorded the song "Luckenbach, Texas" with Waylon Jennings. On any given weekend, you'll find bankers and bikers, young and old country fans milling around, tossing washers and drinking beer at this Hill Country hideout that consists of a post office, dance hall and beer/souvenir shop. People often just sit outside, strumming guitars and singing along. The toughest thing about Luckenbach is finding it. Signs directing people to the town are often stolen by tourists.

THE CIRCLE OF LIFE

Pass the Salad and Hold the Croutons!

Everything is big in Texas—including Texans. According to the Texas Department of Health (now the Department of State Health Services), between 1991 and 2001, the prevalence of obesity among adults in Texas rose from 13 percent to almost 25 percent. During 2001, officials estimate that out of the over 15 million adults living in the state, 36 percent were overweight and 24 percent were obese! While no one is holding the state dish of chicken-fried steak directly responsible for the extra pounds on more than one-third of Texans, health department officials might consider an eating "lite" tax break. The direct cost for obesity in Texas was estimated at $5.8 billion in 2003.

It's the Fries that Getcha'

All those pounds weigh heavy on Texas hearts. In 2003, the Department of State Health Services reported that the biggest killer of Texans was cardiovascular disease. It's the leading cause of death for all ethnic groups, although heart attacks and strokes affect more whites than Hispanics. Hispanics have the state's highest rate of diabetes—nearly twice as high as the state average. African Americans have the lowest accidental death rate; Hispanics have the highest.

Heaven Can't Wait

Texans are passing on to the great Lone Star State in the sky at a rate of 317 per 100,000 people. Texans have the 30th longest life expectancy in the nation, according to a Harvard study. On average, Texans can expect to live until they're 76.7 years old.

Adding New Texans Every Day

In 2003, there were over 377,000 births in Texas. Over 30 percent of those young Texans were born to unmarried mothers. The state's fertility rate was 76.7 per 1000 women between the ages of 15 and 44.

She Looked a Little Young...

Texas had the highest rate of teen pregnancies in 2003 in the nation, with a teen becoming pregnant every 10 minutes. More than 5 percent of the babies that year were born to mothers younger than 18.

Of Course, Where There Are Babies...

With all those new Texans coming into the picture, it only makes sense that the state ranks at the top with STDs or sexually transmitted diseases. Texas reports that sexually transmitted diseases—everything from AIDS down to chlamydia—occur at rate of over 430 per 100,000 adults.

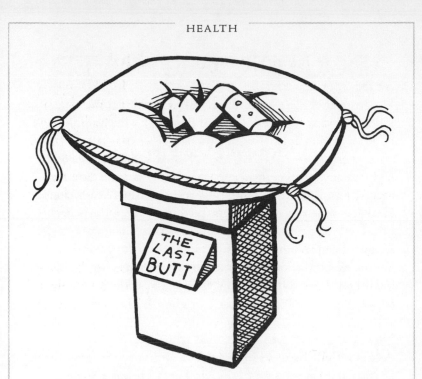

When the Smoke Clears...

Memories of the Marlboro Man still linger in Texas, where the most frequent type of cancer is lung cancer. The good news is that Texans, like the rest of Americans, are kicking the habit. In fact, in Austin, the self-proclaimed live music capital of the world (which generally translates into lots and lots of bars), smoking was banned in 2005 in all restaurants and bars, requiring band members and audience members to step outside for a smoke and making it more dangerous to be standing outside a bar than inside—at least if you plan on inhaling.

DOCTOR, YOU SAVED MY LIFE!

Scraping the Pipes

The first successful carotid endarterectomy (a procedure to remove plaque from the linings of arteries that have developed blockages of fatty deposits) happened in Texas. Dr. Michael Ellis DeBakey, a medical pioneer in cardiovascular surgery, performed the operation in 1953 in Houston at the Baylor University College of Medicine. The procedure is used to reduce the risk of stroke. Dr. DeBakey was on the cover of *Time* magazine in 1965.

Now That's Going to Leave a Mark
If you ever suffer a really deep cut, then you might want to thank a Texan as it's being stitched up. Dr. Hugh Hampton Young, who was born in San Antonio, developed the "boomerang needle," a surgical needle used for working with deep incisions.

Sometimes It's the Little Things

Texas is the only state with three Nobel laureates actively researching nanotechnology. At Rice University, the fullerene form of carbon was discovered in 1985. This discovery inspired the first nanoscale science work, and some of the medical applications of nanotechnology have centered in Dallas. The Blount Laboratoy at UT Southwestern Medical Center is exploring "the action of mechanosensitve changes—gateways at the cellular level that will sense changes in the membrane surface tension." If you can decipher that, there's a lab coat waiting for you in Texas.

Now If He Can Just Make It Taste Better…
Dr. Nicholas Peppas, a University of Texas chemical engineering professor who is considered the father of modern drug delivery, has worked on taking the sting out of taking your medicine. In 1999, he published a report on a form of insulin that could be swallowed instead of injected—something he continues to work on as of the writing of this book. He also developed contact lenses that you only have to replace once a week.

Do You Know Your HDL Level?

If you're busy fretting over your cholesterol medicine, you can blame Dr. Michael S. Brown and Dr. Joseph L. Goldstein. Working at UT Southwestern in Dallas, they discovered the basic mechanism of cholesterol and won the 1985 Nobel Prize. Thanks to their research, there has been considerable development of cholesterol-lowering drugs. So go ahead! Order that chicken-fried steak and fried okra!

PATIENT CARE

It Hurts When I Do This...
If you're going to get sick, Houston is the place to be. It's home to the Texas Medical Center, the world's largest concentration of research and health care institutions—45 in total. All of them are non-profit. There are 13 hospitals, two medical schools, four nursing schools, a cancer center, a children's hospital, a hospice center and 11 different academic and research institutions. The Texas Medical Center (TMC) is also the home of the first and largest air emergency service.

TMC by the Numbers

In 2004, there were over five million patient visits to TMC, more than 10,000 international patients and 27 million square feet of space. There are 6344 beds and 373 bassinets. There are 44,188 parking spaces—no doubt many are reserved for the 4000 physicians or 73,600 other employees (as of 2006). From 2000 to 2004, the Texas Medical Center had $3.5 billion committed to research. More heart surgeries are performed at the Texas Medical Center than anywhere else in the world.

UNIVERSITY OF TEXAS

Learning Large

The University of Texas is the largest university system in the state. The school has nine different campuses: UT El Paso, UT Arlington, UT Brownsville, UT Dallas, UT San Antonio, UT Pan American, UT Permian Basin, UT Tyler and UT Austin.

UT Austin (the original, known simply as UT) is not only the largest in the state, it had the largest enrollment of any university in the country from 1997 to 2003. It awards 12,000 degrees annually, has 900 registered student organizations, 39,000 undergraduates and 450,000 living alumni.

Now That's a Bull!

UT's mascot is Bevo, the Texas longhorn. There have been many Bevos; the most recent, Bevo XIII, was a veteran of 16 seasons, including the university's big 12 win and the season the team's star running back Ricky Williams won the Heisman Trophy. Bevo XIII's most famous moment came after a UT lost to Nebraska in 1999. As he was walking off the field, nature called, and the longhorn left a memento squarely on the Cornhuskers logo.

The Texas Tower Sniper

On August 1, 1966, UT architecture student, former Marine and Eagle Scout Charles Whitman, who had killed both his mother and wife the day before, negotiated his way up to the top of the university's clock tower. Whitman carried with him a 12-gauge shotgun, two rifles, a 30-caliber M-1 carbine and two pistols, several knives, a hatchet and a machete, along with food, water and other supplies.

From the tower deck, starting at 11:48 AM, Whitman opened fire. Using waterspouts on each side of the tower as turrets, which allowed him to continue shoot while largely protected from return gunfire, Whitman killed 14 people and wounded 31 that afternoon. He fired unimpeded for 96 minutes before two Austin police officers climbed the tower and killed him.

An autopsy revealed that Whitman had a cancerous brain tumor. There's been some speculation that because of its location in his brain, it may have caused his behavior to become violent and may even have been somewhat responsible for the attacks. The shooting was considered by many as the impetus for establishing SWAT teams to deal with situations beyond normal police procedures.

Tibet Meets the Pass of the North

The University of Texas at El Paso (popularly known as UTEP) was once known as the Texas State School of Mines and Metallurgy—a mineshaft still exists on campus. Despite the fact the university is located in the desert mountain region of the state known for pueblo-style architecture, the buildings on campus are modeled after a style more common in the eastern Himalayas. And it's largely the fault of *National Geographic*. Kathleen Worrell, writer, artist and wife of the dean, saw photographs of *dzongs*, or fortresses, in Bhutan in the April 1914 issue of the magazine. She was struck by the similarity between the landscape of Bhutan and the Franklin Mountains of El Paso. When the original campus on the military base of Fort Bliss burned down in 1916 and the university was given 23 acres on a mesa north of downtown, she proposed Bhutanese architecture.

The buildings have massive sloping walls and overhanging roofs. Windows are narrow and inaccessible from the ground. Combined with tile and brick just below the roof line, the buildings take on an oddly contemporary look for a campus built in a 12th-century style. It's the only place in the Western Hemisphere where you'll find Bhutanese architecture—except that unlike true Bhutanese methods, construction at UTEP involved both nails and blueprints.

Several Bhutanese students have attended UTEP, and today, the campus has an active art exchange program with Bhutan. Most recently, in 2003 the people of Bhutan gave the university a large, decorated prayer wheel made from cedar and constructed, as is all true Bhutanese architecture, without nails or plans.

DID YOU KNOW?

UTEP is celebrated as the first campus in the nation to integrate its intercollegiate athletic teams. In 1966, when the campus was known as Texas Western, basketball coach Don Haskins took his team to the NCAA Men's Basketball Championship with an all-black starting lineup, thus breaking an unspoken barrier and changing the history of college basketball. The story was chronicled in the movie *Glory Road*.

TEXAS AGRICULTURAL AND MECHANICAL COLLEGE

The Aggies

Texas A&M was the state's first public institution of higher education and is UT's main rival. It opened in 1876 as the Agricultural and Mechanical College of Texas. In the early 1900s, A&M students were referred to as farmers, but the term Aggie began in 1920. In 1949, the yearbook changed its name to *Aggieland*, and Aggies, became the official name for the student body.

Standing By

Texas A&M is best known for its traditions, of which the most famous is the Twelfth Man. In a 1922 football game against Centre College, the A&M team suffered injury after injury, seriously

depleting their bench. Coach Dana X. Bible, worrying that he'd be out of players at the rate the game was going, had an idea. He knew a former football player was at the game. E. King Gill was called from the stands and suited up, and he stood ready throughout the rest of the game, which A&M finally won 22–14. When the game ended, E. King Gill was the only man left standing on the sidelines for the Aggies. Gill said, "I wish I could say that I went in and ran for the winning touchdown, but I did not. I simply stood by in case my team needed me."

He came to be thought of as the Twelfth Man because he stood ready for duty in the event that the 11 men on the gridiron needed assistance. Now the entire student body at A&M is the Twelfth Man, and they stand during the entire game to show their support. There is even a statue of Gill on campus, making him the only athlete memorialized for not playing.

Did You Hear the One…

There are few things more Texas than Aggie jokes. Aggie jokes are the blond jokes of Texas. Most of the best ones come from Texas A&M alumni. Here are a few tried and true:

☛ Question: Why do Aggies hate M&Ms?

Answer: They're too hard to peel.

☛ An Aggie was down on his luck. In order to raise some money he decided to kidnap a kid and hold him for ransom. He went to the playground, grabbed a kid, took him behind a tree and told him, "I've kidnapped you."

The Aggie quickly scribbled a ransom note: "I've kidnapped your kid. Tomorrow morning, put $10,000 in a paper bag and put it beneath the pecan tree next to the slide on the north side of the city playground. Signed, an Aggie." The Aggie then pinned the note to the kid's shirt and sent him home to show it to his parents.

The next morning the Aggie checked, and sure enough a paper bag was sitting beneath that pecan tree. The Aggie opened up the bag and found the $10,000 with a note. The note said, "How could one Aggie do this to another Aggie?"

☛ Did you hear that there aren't any cold drinks at A&M anymore?

The girl with the recipe for ice graduated.

☛ Question: What do you call a smart person on the A&M campus?

Answer: A visitor.

☛ There are three types of Aggies—those who can count and those who can't.

☛ Question: How many Aggies does it take to screw in a lightbulb?

Answer: One, but he gets three hours credit.

☛ Did you hear that the A&M library had to close down this year?

Somebody stole the book. And that's not all; when it was returned, it was all colored in.

☛ A guy walks into a bar and says to the bartender, "Hey bartender, I know a great Aggie joke. You want to hear it?"

The bartender says, "Well, before you tell it I should probably tell you that I went to A&M. And you see those two big guys sitting next to you—they were linebackers for the A&M football team. And those two guys on your other side—they're Marines, and they used to be in the Corps of Cadets at A&M. Now, are you sure you really want to tell that Aggie joke?"

The guy thinks for a second. "I guess not," he says. "I wouldn't want to have to explain it five times."

TTU, TSU, UNT AND RICHLAND

Who Is That Masked Man?

Texas Tech University in Lubbock is home of the Red Raiders. The Masked Rider, originally known as the "Ghost Rider," was an unofficial mascot starting around 1936, when an unknown student would circle the field on horseback at home football games, riding into the stadium and then riding away. A few stitches, a cool hat and voila, the Masked Rider became the official mascot in 1954.

The Tale of the Tail

A statue of Will Rogers and his horse, Soapsuds, stands on the Texas Tech campus. According to local legend, the statue, which was donated by a long-time friend of Rogers, was meant to be pointing west so that Rogers and his horse would be headed for the sunset (as is said on the plaque attached to the base). However, facing the sunset would have meant the horse's tail end would be pointed toward downtown, which would have sent a, well, mixed message to the university's supportive business community. Another adjustment considered would have sent an equally insulting message to the administrative office. Instead, horse and rider were adjusted 23° to the northwest, so that today, Soapsuds' rear end is perpetually pointed towards Texas A&M.

We're All Normal Here

Texas State University in San Marcos opened its doors in 1903 as Southwest Texas State Normal School. The school was primarily a teachers' college, and the term "normal" doesn't refer to the student body. It was a word often used by teaching colleges that meant teaching to the "norms" or guidelines. After four name changes, Texas State University is now the state's sixth largest university and the largest in Texas' state university system.

DID YOU  KNOW?

The most famous graduate of Texas State University in San Marcos is U.S. President Lyndon Baines Johnson. Texas State has the distinction of being the only major university in Texas to have a U.S. president among its alumni.

Where Squirrels Rule—Almost

The University of North Texas (more commonly called North Texas) is in Denton. It is the largest university in northern Texas and the fourth largest in the state. The university was founded in 1890 as Texas Normal College and Teacher Training Institute. Among other things, the university features the first jazz studies program in the U.S., which is consistently ranked the nation's best.

The North Texas mascot, an eagle, was adopted in 1922. In the spring of 2002, the school's chapter of the Albino Squirrel Preservation Society attempted to make the albino squirrel the school's secondary mascot, but although the vote was close, the eagle remained the only mascot. Ironically, in August 2006, the albino squirrel that was believed to bring luck to students who spotted him before an exam was killed by a hawk—a victim of his own lack of camouflage.

Things That Go Boom

North Texas is also home to Boomer, a 2:3 scale, six-pound M1841 cannon that has been fired every time the Mean Green have scored since the fall of 1970. In 1996, the U.S. Field Artillery Association inspected the cannon and indicated that was unsafe to fire. After a quick shopping trip, a second cannon, Boomer II, was brought to North Texas and has been faithfully firing in Boomer I's place.

If Not a Squirrel, How About a Duck?

Not many community colleges have a mascot, but Richland College in Dallas does—Thunderduck. It's unclear why Richland adopted a mascot of a duck carrying a thunderbolt, although the campus, which has a brook flowing through it and is on what used to be the old Jackson farm, is home to many, many ducks. Faculty will often warn visitors to watch their step.

LIVING IN TEXAS

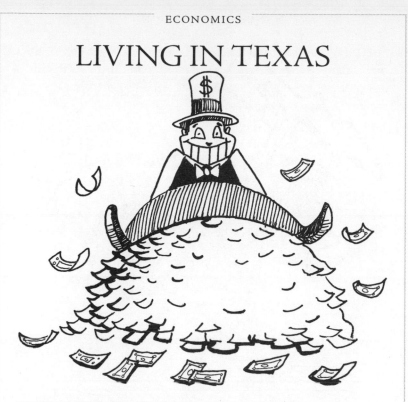

Do You Think We Could Have Our Own Currency?

As of 2004, if Texas was a nation—well, it practically is, but that's another story—it would have the eighth largest economy in the world. The comptroller was forecasting a $924 billion gross state product for 2005. As of 2005, Texas ranks 14th in the nation for personal income. Who's making the most? The highest incomes appear to belong to folks living in the Dallas and Houston areas.

Pack Your Bags and Your Savings Account

The cost of living in Texas varies widely. An individual moving from Riverside, California, with a salary of $65,000 could get by with a pay cut down to $51,000 and still maintain the status quo in San Angelo, Texas. But if that person were to move to Austin, he or she would need a bump in salary to $81,000.

Still, all of the cities in Texas rank below the average cost of living in the U.S., some significantly more than others. El Paso is just over eight percent below the average, and Dallas is a little more than four percent below.

I'll Take Four Bedrooms and a Pool—Outside of Town

Several Texas cities, such as Odessa, Waco, Wichita Falls and Brownsville, have the lowest-priced housing around, but you can expect to pay a good bit more in the major metropolitan areas. Austin's median home prices are the highest in the state—which may explain why traffic into the capital city is so bogged down.

WORKING IN TEXAS

How Can I Help You?

The type of work happening in the state has changed dramatically. The service sector in the state has grown to 20 percent of the Texas GSP (gross state product) in 2001 while manufacturing and mining have fallen to 6.2 percent of the GSP in 2001, down from 19.6 percent in 1981.

I Have an Idea!

Texas residents are busy thinking of the next big thing. According to the U.S. Patent and Trademark Office, Texans were issued 5660 patents and filed 12,951 patent applications in 2005, enough for second in the nation in both categories behind California. In 2004, the National Science Foundation ranked Texas third in the nation for academic research and development spending— the state poured $2.8 billion into R&D.

DID YOU KNOW?

In 2004, Galveston County was reported by the *Houston Business Journal* as the best county in which to test a new product.

Getting It Correct

Bette Nesmith Graham, a divorced single mother and freelance artist, invented Liquid Paper. It all started in 1951 when Graham took a secretarial job to make ends meet and took to carefully painting over her mistakes. She whipped up the first batch of "mistake out" in her kitchen blender. By 1975, her company employed 200 people, made 25 million bottles of the correctional fluid and was available in 31 countries. Graham sold the company to Gillette in 1979 for $47.5 million.

DID YOU KNOW?

Graham's son, Michael Nesmith, helped his mother by filling bottles for customers. He later launched the band the Monkees.

A Fertile Imagination

When Bill Black, an Austin-area barber in the 1970s, noticed how hair clippings, which fell onto plants near his barber chair, seemingly improved their growth, he did a little research. He learned that hair contained 18 percent nitrogen and, since plant

fertilizer is nitrogen based, the clippings he'd been casually tossing in the dustbin might be better put to use as plant fertilizer.
With that, he launched FertHairLizer—a plant fertilizer product that's still being sold today.

PAYING TAXES IN TEXAS

Tax Free...Sort of

Texas has no personal income tax. None. Nada. It's actually prohibited by the Texas Constitution. Well, it's not completely banned, but it is so restricted that it's practically impossible to pass, not to mention political suicide. Basically, a personal income tax would have to be ratified in a statewide referendum to take effect. Texas' constitution also prohibits statewide property taxes. Instead, the state raises revenue through sales taxes and a recently enacted (2006) gross receipts tax on businesses.

Tax-Free Weekend

Every year, Texas has a sales tax holiday. That's right, sales taxes in Texas are lifted temporarily—for back-to-school shopping. For three whole days, a wide variety of items seen as somehow related to the category of "school supplies" are tax-free. One glance at the list of taxed and not taxed items below and you'll wonder what kind of bizarre logic is at work when the legislature considers baby clothes a back-to-school item, but not backpacks.

Tax Free	Taxed
athletic socks	backpacks
baby clothes	barrettes, ponytail holders
belts	bicycle shoes, bowling shoes
coats	boots
baseball, football jerseys	golf gloves
pajamas	football pants
sweaters	helmets, hard hats
swimsuits	ice skates
underclothes	safety clothing, glasses
work clothes	zippers, buttons

TRANSPORTATION IN TEXAS

The Hub of Texas

☛ The Dallas/Fort Worth Airport, known simply as DFW, is larger than Manhattan. The facility covers nearly 30 square miles and is the largest airport in the state, the second largest in the U.S. and the third largest in the world in terms of operations.

☛ DFW has its own zip code (75261, in case you were wondering).

☛ The airport is the hub for American Airlines, which has 800 departures a day, but nearly every other airline flies in and out of DFW.

☛ Given this busy schedule, there are seven runways, the longest of which is 13,400 feet long, and three FAA control towers.

☛ In 1972, it took three million yards of concrete to pave the airport's initial runways.

☛ There are 174 gates and five terminals.

☛ In 2005, over 59 million passengers made their way through DFW.

☛ Within the airport is the largest airport high-speed train, Skylink. High speed is relative, though. The completely automated Skylink trains run every few minutes at speeds up to 37 miles per hour.

☛ The first time the supersonic Concorde landed in the U.S., it landed at DFW in 1973. The airport had just been completed, though it wasn't open for commercial operations when the Concorde touched down. The gates on the largest and, at the time, costliest airport were officially opened on January 13, 1974.

☛ Becoming a mammoth airport wasn't all clear skies for DFW. Surrounding cities at one point sued in an attempt to restrain its growth. The U.S. Supreme Court decided the case in 1994 in favor of the airport. Two years later, DFW added its seventh runway.

Are We There Yet?

Texas has the country's biggest highway system, with over 79,000 miles of state-maintained roads (as of 2005; more are being paved all the time), 101 rest areas and 743 picnic areas. Texas also has more road signs than any other state. There are over half a million signs on state-maintained highways. And that doesn't include billboards.

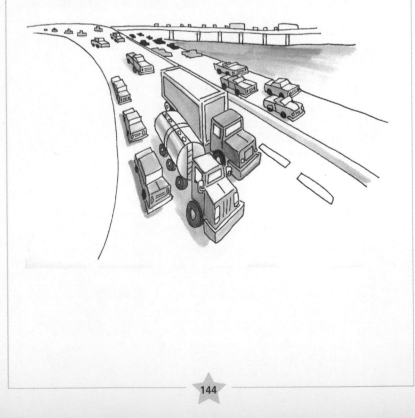

Texas U-turns, or Texas turn-arounds, were invented in Texas. These allow cars traveling on one side of a one-way frontage road to U-turn under or over a freeway to go the opposite way on the other frontage road without stopping at lights or intersections. Most Texas freeways also have dual frontage roads running parallel on each side, feeding traffic in from individual city and rural streets.

I Told You to Go Before We Left!

Busier than some hotel chains, Texas rest areas are visited by 50 million travelers annually. Some are full-blown tourist destinations in and of themselves, with the Texas Department of Transportation adding wi-fi, large playgrounds and air conditioning to its rest areas.

DID YOU KNOW?

The art-deco style comes alive in Donley County Eastbound rest area, where the lobby conveniently contains a tornado shelter.

Football Practice is Called Off on Account of Heavy Traffic

It's nice to know that someone out there spends time worrying about the possibility of falling trucks in Texas. The Texas Highway Institute at Texas A&M developed a special heavy-duty, extra-tall guardrail for a downtown San Antonio freeway ramp to prevent heavy trucks from crashing down onto a local high school football field below. To test the guardrail, they crashed a fully loaded tanker truck into it. To date, no trucks have hit the field, and practice goes on.

Hey Kids!
Don't mess
with Texas!

Tough Trash Talking

GSD&M, a big ad firm in Austin, gave the Texas Department
of Transportation (TxDOT) the most ridiculously popular anti-
litter campaign to hit the highway. "Don't Mess With Texas"
has practically become a state motto. The campaign featured
a wide variety of Texas celebrities, including late guitar legend
Stevie Ray Vaughn, Willie Nelson, Matthew McConaughey,
LeAnn Rimes, Ian Moore, George Foreman and Lance
Armstrong, scowling at the camera and saying "Don't mess with
Texas." TxDOT now has a serious side business selling "Don't
Mess With Texas" hats, bags, stickers, magnets, etc. And you
can report a litterbug on the website. The offender won't get
a ticket, though. Just a free trash bag.

How many times have you been driving and said to yourself, "Now *here's* a pretty stretch of road looking for a home." The Adopt-a-Highway program started in Texas, saving the state over $4 million in trash pick-up costs. The state provides bags, reflective vests and signs telling drivers to slow down. Volunteers provide the litter-picking muscle. All kinds of groups adopt highways, including families, community groups, businesses and even the Texas Camel Corps. The Adopt-a-Highway program is now in 49 states, Canada, Puerto Rico, New Zealand, Australia and Japan.

Slow Down and Smell the Bluebonnets!

Wildflowers are a big deal along the highways in the Texas Hill Country, thanks to the much-beloved Lady Bird Johnson, wife of president Lyndon Baines Johnson. Lady Bird, who got her nickname at an early age when a nursemaid said she was "as purty as a lady bird," spearheaded highway beautification. She had always admired the wildflowers in the Texas Hill Country and believed they could be preserved. Thanks to her efforts, the Texas Department of Transportation has been busy planting wildflowers and native plants since the 1920s. For years, Lady Bird gave a $1000 prize to the person in the highway department who did the best job. Texas sows from 30,000 to 60,000 pounds of flower seeds (most of them bluebonnets) along highways every year. The TxDOT Travel Division even has a Wildflower Information Hotline to help people find the most colorful patches of highway.

DID YOU  KNOW?

Each year, 140 million cigarette butts are tossed out on Texas highways. It can take 20 years for a butt to decompose.

With all that driving, it shouldn't be surprising that there is a tread problem in Texas. After all, those tires have to go somewhere after they leave all that rubber on the road. Where they go is Atlanta, Texas. Atlanta is home to the largest scrap tire stockpile in the country. In 2002, the stockpile covered approximately 150 acres and contained more than 30 million shredded and whole tires. It got to the point that it was considered an environmental hazard. By 2005, cleanup efforts had the pile down to 18 million shredded and whole tires. That's progress.

Honey, Smile After that 18-Wheeler Goes By

Every Texas Hill Country child has done his or her time on the side of a highway in a field of bluebonnets while his or her parents risk life and limb to get the traditional spring photo. And while the children will trample hundreds of the flowers during their posing, their parents will shout the familiar refrain, "Don't pick the bluebonnets! It's illegal!" Like so many things parents tell young children, it's not true, according to the Texas Department of Transportation. They should know.

SMALL PRODUCTS, BIG INDUSTRIES

Not Just Cattle and Oil

There are two classic images of Texas' economy: cows being watched over by cowboys on horseback and oil wells bursting with thick, black oil. While most Texans live their entire lives without seeing either one outside of a museum exhibit, the images are based on two very real major financial forces in the state. Of course, Texas has a few other industries making money, tourism and technology being two of the most important.

Even Little Things Are Big in Texas

Most venture capitalists in Texas aren't looking for oil or cattle in the state these days; they're far more interested in the little things in life. Mainly they're investing in silicone and software. Texas ranks number two in the nation for the number of employees working in the semiconductor industry and number one in the nation for the total capital investment in the sector. The major employers in the semiconductor business in the state are Texas Instruments in Dallas, Raytheon in Garland, Freescale and Advanced Micro Devices in Austin and Labinal (aerospace and electrical) in Corinth. The value of industry exports is $13.3 billion annually.

Is There a Pill for That?

Pharmaceuticals are big business in Texas. In 2005, pharmaceuticals was Texas' second largest exporting category, right behind semiconductors and computers. There are 110 pharmaceutical firms in the state, employing nearly 10,000 workers.

TOURISM

Coming to Texas

As the Lyle Lovett song goes, "That's right you're not from Texas, Texas wants you anyway." And folks are hearing the message and heading to the state, at least for a week or so. Texas tourism is a big-dollar industry, with an estimated 70 percent of the 203 million travelers to Texas coming for pleasure, not business. In 2005, the total of direct travel spending was $49.2 billion, and both the state and localities scored $3.4 billion in revenue from travel spending. About 10 percent of visitors were international. Another 40 percent were from other states. Then there are the locals...

Texans Love to Visit Texas

Actually, Texas residents accounted for one-half of all visitor spending in the state in 2005. When you consider that it can take an entire day just to drive across the state—assuming you need breaks to sleep and eat—it's understandable. Going from one end of Texas to the other is like going from Providence, Rhode Island, to Charlotte, North Carolina (you'll hit seven states in the process). You can go from beaches to desert to swampland in the state. You can hike canyons and plains or water-ski on one of the state's many man-made lakes.

Come On In and Stay a While

Here's a question for you. When are tourists not tourists? When they are Winter Texans. These snowbirds flock to Texas around November, their RVs bearing the signs of their native habitats: Wisconsin, Michigan, Iowa. They settle in to wait out winter in the mild southern and Rio Grande Valley areas of the state. Back in 1997, their numbers were estimated at 1.3 million, and they are welcomed to their winter roost with considerable enthusiasm using billboards, yard signs and newspapers. And it's no wonder everyone is so happy to see them coming. Winter Texans inject nearly one billion dollars into the state's economy. The vast majority of Winter Texans stay in RV parks, volunteer for local non-profit organizations and make numerous trips into Mexico. Some become embroiled in local politics. In 2000, a group of RVers in East Texas, known as the Escapees, made headlines fighting for the ability to vote in local elections.

CATTLE

See What Happens When You Leave Them Alone?

The longhorn gets a great deal of the credit for Texas' rebound after the Civil War. Texas longhorn cattle, having been largely left to themselves while their owners took part in the Civil War, spent their time doing what comes natural in the rolling plains of Texas. The result was huge herds, an estimated three to six million head, roaming across the state. With such a surplus of cattle, the price of beef in the state plummeted to $2 per head. But a few folks figured out that those same bovines were worth $40 a head up north, where wartime demand had wiped out cattle herds. Suddenly, delivering cattle hundreds of miles away seemed like a very good idea.

The cattle drive is a Texas invention. Edward Piper drove 1000 cattle to Ohio in 1846. By the 1850s, a Texas cow, worth $14 in the state, was bringing $100 in California's gold rush country. Cattle drives really caught on after the Civil War, though. In 1866 alone, Texans drove more than 260,000 head of cattle all over the U.S. The Texas longhorn was uniquely suited to cattle drives because of its long legs and hard hoofs. Each day, wranglers would travel about 10 miles, letting cattle graze as they went. Cattle drives had another impact on the state. They created a whole new area for myth and legend to mix, plus a whole host of catchy cattle drive songs. "Home on the Range" is probably the most famous.

Just Be Careful Crossing the Street...

Fort Worth is known in Texas as "Cowtown," and for good reason. Every day, twice a day, there's a longhorn cattle drive right down the middle of Exchange Avenue in the Stockyards District. The stockyards in Fort Worth were the center of the cattle trade in the late 1800s, and while cars outnumber cows these days, the Old West manages to hold on in that city. In addition to the daily cattle drives (11:30 AM and 4:00 PM), there are western shops, weekend rodeos and two museums celebrating both the men and women of cattle country: the Texas Cowboys Hall of Fame and the National Cowgirl Hall of Fame.

Where's the Posse When You Need It?

Cattle are still routinely branded for the same reason as they were hundreds of years ago—to stop cattle rustlers. Not much has changed about the process. Branding irons are still just metal heated up, and brands are still burned into cattle. Horses are sometime freeze-branded instead, which is less painful and, instead of leaving a scar, causes the hair in the area to grow in white. Either way, the only high-tech part of the whole thing is that brands are now recorded on computers. Modern cattle rustling is a major problem for ranchers in Texas. In 2006, rustlers made off with 5500 head of cattle and other equipment from ranches in Texas and Oklahoma, resulting in losses of $6.5 million. A single trailerload of cattle can give a thief a $20,000 payoff. To combat the problem, ranchers have instituted Internet alerts, increased the number of investigators in feedlots and launched Operation Cow Thief, which offers a 24-hour hotline and reward money for information on cattle thieves.

Moooove on Over!

Texas raises far more cattle than any other state—15 million head, according to the state's comptroller. While known for their longhorns, Texas ranchers also raise Angus, Brahman, Charolais, Hereford and dozens of other varieties of beef and dairy cattle. A 1000-pound heifer will yield 432 pounds of beef—and 18 pairs of shoes.

DID YOU KNOW?

In 1995, cattle production in Texas brought in more dollars than natural gas production. The industry contributes over $15 billion annually to the state's economy, according to a Texas A&M 2001 report.

It's Not Just Fertilizer Anymore

Fifteen million head of cattle also means fifteen million tails of cattle. And what comes out of the tail end of a cow is becoming a valuable source of renewable energy. A 1000-pound cow produces 10 tons of manure a year. Some experts hope that in a few years, cow manure will compete with natural gas head to head, so to speak. The state's energy conservation office is encouraging feedlots and dairies to burn dry manure as "biomass energy." In fact, Hereford, Texas, is home to the largest biomass-fueled ethanol refinery in the U.S. While dry manure is being used to refine ethanol, research is underway to turn the "higher water content" manure (we just call it "fresh") into biogas and, eventually, methane.

Just Take These Magazines and Moo When You're Done
Bull semen is a big business in Texas. Longhorn bull semen is even available online and can be frozen for up to 50 years for later use. A champion bull's semen can garner over a million dollars, and scouts in the semen business are always on the lookout at state rodeos and ranches for new champions to...well, um, "collect" from.

The King Ranch in Texas is the largest ranch in the world and is even bigger than Rhode Island. It would take days to get across the ranch on horseback. With 825,000 acres, it spans six counties. It all started when Richard King and Gideon K. Lewis set up a cattle camp on Santa Gertrudis Creek in 1852. They started out with a Spanish land grant of 15,500 acres, which cost them $300, then added another 53,000 acres for $1800; then they got really serious. After a whole tangle of land acquisitions in the decade following Lewis' death in 1855, the ranch grew to epic proportions, both in land and legend. For a while, it was actually 1.2 million acres—about the size of Grand Canyon National Park!

Now Hiring

Richard King moved the entire population of the Mexican village Cruillas, which had been devastated by drought, to the ranch to work on the land. He had just bought their cattle, which they had sold in desperation to survive, and was on his way home when he realized that the people in the village no longer had a livelihood. He turned back and offered them food, shelter and income. They became known as *kineños*, or "King's men." Many of the descendants of the original Cruillas villagers still work and live on the ranch.

That'll Leave a Mark

Longhorns, Brahman and the famous Santa Gertrudis cattle (which were recognized as a breed in 1940) are all raised on the King Ranch. The ranch's brand, the "running W," is nearly as famous as the ranch. Its history is murky, though. Some people say it's based on the wriggling moves of a diamondback rattlesnake (there are plenty on the ranch); others say it's meant to look like the sweep of a longhorn's horns. Or it could be an abstract form to unite the past and the present with the future. In any case, its design allows the wound to heal quickly, and the brand grows with the animal that has it. Whatever it was supposed to stand for, these days one thing is for sure—in Texas, it means King Ranch.

When the Going Gets Tough, Drill for Oil

In the 1920s and '30s, the King Ranch went through tough times. The matriarch of the family, Henrietta King, died in 1925. Then the ranch faced difficult financial times because of poor beef market conditions. Like so many Texans, the ranch was saved by oil. Today, the King Ranch has expanded to 60,000 head of cattle in Arizona, Kentucky, Florida, Brazil and Texas. It's ranked 175th out of the top 500 businesses in the state, and the ranch even has its own museum in—where else—Kingsville.

DID YOU KNOW?

The television series *Dallas* made another, much smaller, Texas ranch famous—Southfork. Now a resort and convention center, Southfork was a working ranch north of Dallas when the series chose the white mansion as the site for production. The 200-acre ranch became a tourist mecca, eventually driving the ranch's family to turn the place into an actual tourist attraction instead of a home. The family sold the ranch to an Arizona businessman and headed for greener, quieter pastures.

OIL

Eww, What's That on Your Foot?

Texas has been leaking oil for hundreds of years. Luis de Moscoso, who had been forced ashore near Sabine Pass during an early expedition in 1543, reported seeing oil floating on the surface of the water. Settlers and visitors commonly observed seepages of crude oil in the early 1800s. So there was no doubt that there was something going on under all that brush and prairie grass. When Spindletop blew and produced 17 million barrels in 1902, the first Texas oil boom was born. Over 100 years later, Texas remains the largest oil and gas producer in the country.

DID YOU KNOW?

Before it was an oil well, Spindletop was a hill formed by a giant underground dome of salt. Native Americans in the area had seen oil seepages in the area for centuries and used the tar to treat various ailments. By 1903, more than 400 wells were drilled into the dome.

The Numbers

Texas produces 350 million barrels of crude oil per year. There are 26 refineries in Texas, most along the Gulf Coast. Crude oil is used for everything from fuel to lotion, but mostly fuel: 45 percent of crude oil is made into gasoline, 21 percent into home heating or diesel and nine percent into jet fuel. The remaining oil is made into other fuels as well as asphalt, petrochemical feedstocks and lubricants.

The Baytown Refinery is the largest oil refinery in the U.S. It opened for production in 1919, takes up 2400 acres and handles 557,000 barrels of crude per day. As large as Baytown is, it's still surprising that during two of its large expansions, one in 1988 and another in 1989, no one in the regulatory world noticed until 2000. Most locals who complained about the expansion sold their homes to the company and moved.

Crude (Oil) Talk

There are all kinds of interesting bits of jargon in the oil business. Here's a sample:

☛ Brine well: Many of the places you'll find oil, you'll also find salt. Drillers dissolve the salt by injecting fresh water into the formations, then pumping it back to the surface as saturated sodium chloride brine—really salty water—which is then used in petrochemical refineries and other related operations.

☛ Christmas tree: Out in the oil fields, this may be the closest you ever get to a pine tree. An oil field Christmas tree refers to the tangle of pipes, valves, gauges and equipment from the ground up that handles the flow of gas.

☛ Pig: A pig is a device stuck into pipelines to check for leaks, obstructions and other maintenance activities. It is pushed through with water, oil or some other pipeline product and looks nothing like a pig, really. It's called a pig, or so the legend goes, because of the squealing sound the device makes as it squeezes through the pipeline.

 Oil and gas drilling is a dangerous business, as the late Texan Red Adair could attest. Red developed most modern day wild well control—or oil field fire fighting—techniques. Using a combination of explosives, mud and concrete, Red and his team put out over 2000 fires. The Red Adair Company became internationally famous in 1962 when they snuffed the 450-foot-high pillar of flame in the Sahara known as the "Devil's Cigarette Lighter." Adair was also famous for being the first person to cap an underwater wild well and for putting out 117 fires in Kuwait after the first Gulf War. His most famous quote: "If you think it's expensive to hire a professional to do the job, wait until you hire an amateur."

THERE'S LOTS OF SPACE IN TEXAS

Johnson Space Center

The first word uttered on the moon was "Houston." And most Houstonians will be happy to remind everyone of this fact at every opportunity. The exact quote is, "Houston, Tranquility Base here. The Eagle has landed." While Houston is known as a hub for the oil and gas business, NASA's Johnson Space Center is a point of pride. Mission Control for every NASA shuttle flight is in Houston. The Mission Control Center (or MCC, as it's referred to by those in the rockets to space business) also manages all activity on the international space station.

But few people know that Johnson Space Center has a softer side. It's also a wildflower refuge. Johnson Space Center is located where the prairie meets the marsh. Large, undeveloped areas of the space center's 1580 acres are mostly grassland, just as they were before it opened in the 1960s. Not satisfied with testing the limits of space, Johnson Space Center is now a test site for wildflower propagation and sustainable landscaping.

 Johnson Space Center is where astronauts do most of their training, and it's where the big pool is. The Neutral Buoyancy Lab is a 202-foot-long, 40-foot-deep pool with 6.2 million gallons of water. Astronauts practice using all the equipment used in a space walk, including the large station robotic arm and a full-scale working model of the shuttle. These electrically operated tools aren't strong enough to lift themselves on Earth, but in zero gravity they can manipulate tens of thousands of pounds.

Dark Skies

The darkest night skies in Texas are in the mountains of Fort Davis, home to McDonald Observatory. The Hobby-Eberly telescope there has a 9.2-meter (433-inch) mirror and is one of the world's largest optical telescopes. Its specialty is studying the properties of light from stars and galaxies. It's considered ideal for searching for planets and studying distant galaxies, exploding stars, black holes and more. McDonald Observatory also has a laser system that measures the distance between the moon and Earth. The observatory uses a combination of laser ranging with satellites and the moon to track the drift of Earth's continents. Underway at the observatory is the Texas Supernova Search. It's a project aimed at finding exploding stars as quickly as possible after their explosion. As of 2004, 30 supernovae have been found.

Finders, Keepers

In March 1998, seven boys were playing basketball outside a home in Monahans when they heard a series of sonic booms and whistles. Then they heard the impact of a good-sized rock in a nearby vacant lot. They called the authorities, and firefighters confiscated the soccer ball–sized rock, promising to return it to the boys if it wasn't radioactive. As word spread and offers to buy what appeared to be a meteorite came in from universities and collectors, the families of the boys asked for it back. But the city was reluctant to return it; experts had determined it might be worth over $30,000. The mayor sent a letter politely declining to give back the rock because the meteorite had landed on city property. City council met and, sensing the public relations crater as the children hired a lawyer and local media had a field day, they voted to return the rock. Later, scientists discovered microscopic quantities of liquid water trapped in salt crystals in the 4.5-billion-year-old meteorite named Monahans '98 1.

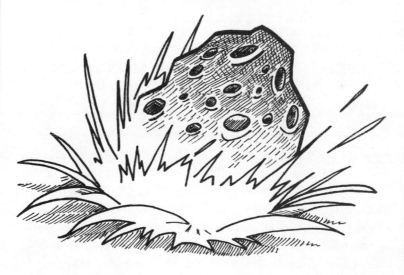

THE LAY OF THE POLITICAL LAND

Red or Blue?
For most of Texas' political history, the state had been a stronghold of the Democratic Party. In fact, Texas was long considered a one-party state, with virtually all races being decided in Democratic primaries, not general elections. Republicans began to turn the tide in the late 1950s. It became increasingly grim for Democrats in the late 1970s. From 1976 through 1992, Texas did not support a single Democratic presidential candidate. In the 1990s, the Republicans gained control of one-third of the Texas congressional delegation, which is a startling turn when you consider that before the 1950s, the Democrats controlled the entire delegation. Now, after a hundred years as the underdogs, Republicans are the dominant political force in the state.

Election Mania
Special elections are called to fill offices when a representative dies or moves up the political food chain. In 1941, 29 candidates entered the fray to replace a long-time senator. But that was nothing. In 1961, there was a total free-for-all when 71 candidates campaigned to replace Senator Johnson.

Spokes-Governor

Texas has what is considered a weak governor structure from a political standpoint. But that hasn't held anyone back from pursuing the state's highest office. Every strategy in the book has been used to secure a four-year stay in the Governor's Mansion in Austin. There was the "shake thousands of hands" approach from Pat Neff, who made 850 campaign appearances in 1920. On the other end of the scale, there was the "shake no hands" approach of Francis R. Lubbock. Lubbock didn't campaign at all in 1861 and still managed to win.

DID YOU **KNOW?**

Texas has allowed candidates to run against themselves. In 1960, Senator Lyndon B. Johnson ran for both senator and vice president. Senator Lloyd Bentsen did the same in 1988.

Red Fever in the Governor's Mansion
Only three governors of Texas have been elected as Republicans: Edmund J. Davis, William P. Clements Jr., and George W. Bush. Rick Perry, also a Republican, was appointed when Bush became president. Perry has gone on to be the longest standing governor in the state.

My, What a Lovely Coat

Texas governors are nothing if not eccentric. Governor William P. Clements wore decidedly bizarre sports coats. Edmund Davis, after losing his re-election bid, barricaded himself inside the governor's office and refused to leave. Stanley Edward Adams, while filing to run for governor in 1990, listed his occupation as "alleged white collar racketeer." "Ma" Ferguson, the first female chief executive, became governor after her husband, "Farmer Jim" Ferguson was impeached. In fact, Jim Ferguson was the first governor in the entire U.S. to be impeached.

DID YOU  KNOW?

The Texas State Legislature meets only every two years for just five months.

The Governor Who Would Be King…or President

George W. Bush defeated incumbent Governor Ann Richards in 1994. He was the first Texas governor to be elected for two consecutive four-year terms, and the first son of a president to be governor. During his tenure, he proclaimed June 10 to be Jesus Day in Texas. He also executed more prisoners than any other governor in history.

His Word Was Law

In Texas, the real power is in the gavel of the lieutenant governor. And no lieutenant governor had more power in his gavel than Bob Bullock. Nearly named the official state fossil of Texas in 1989, Bullock was well known as a workaholic, a Texas-sized Machiavelli and a master of politics. He was described as a man with an explosive temper, one who would ignore common civility and once had a pizza fight with his own staff. Bullock is credited with being the principal architect of modern Texas government. The state's history museum is named after him.

It features a 35-foot bronze star, and the building itself is constructed from sunset red granite from the same quarry as the granite of the Texas Capitol.

When Knowing Nothing was Worth Something

The Know Nothing party entered the Texas political landscape in 1854, a secretive party that got its popular name from its members' pat answer to any question about party activities. Know Nothing candidates carried two large municipal elections. Arguing that both Germans and Mexicans were dangerous to the American way of life, the Know Nothings ended up driving both groups to the Democratic Party. It was a strategic error they never recovered from.

DID YOU  KNOW?

President Millard Fillmore was a Know Nothing gubernatorial candidate in Texas. He was soundly defeated by Democrat James Buchanan. Perhaps it was the name…

WOMEN IN TEXAS POLITICS

A Woman in the Senate

Women have been a driving force in Texas politics, and perhaps no one was more beloved than Barbara Jordan. Jordan was the first African-American woman to be elected to the State Senate, and in 1972 was the first African-American congresswoman from the Deep South. She was famous for her booming oratory.

Famous Quotes from Barbara Jordan

- "Just remember, the world is not a playground but a schoolroom. Life is not a holiday but an education."

- "The American dream is not dead. It is gasping for breath, but it is not dead."

- "If you're going to play the game properly, you'd better know every rule."

- "My faith in the Constitution is whole; it is complete; it is total. I am not going to sit here and be an idle spectator to the diminution, the subversion, the destruction of the Constitution" (spoken during the 1974 Watergate impeachment hearings).

Remaking the Bed and Taking On the Klan

Although Ma Ferguson is generally considered to have been a mere figurehead, pretty much just standing in for her husband, she did take on some tough issues. She openly challenged the Ku Klux Klan, for one. In her campaign, she said, "Let us take the sheets and put them back on the beds!" She eventually passed a law preventing the wearing of masks in public, which was a direct attack on the Klan. Ma Ferguson also appointed three women to sit as special justices on the Texas Supreme Court, making it the only all-female supreme court in any state. And she wouldn't allow drinking or smoking in the Governor's Mansion—likely the first and last time that rule was in effect.

When the Women Were In Charge
When Ann Richards became governor in 1991, women were also mayors of the three largest cities in the state:

☛ Annette Strauss was the first female mayor of Dallas;

☛ Kathryn J. Whitmire was the first female mayor of Houston (and had been the first female elected to Houston city government); and

☛ Lila Cockrell in San Antonio was the first female mayor of any major American city.

A Message From the Fields
Irma L. Rangel was the first Hispanic woman ever to be elected to the Texas State Legislature. She credited her 1976 victory largely to the support of female migrant workers. Before being elected to the Legislature, she was one of the first female Hispanic assistant district attorneys. She passed a bill to create South Texas' first professional school, the College of Pharmacy at Texas A&M in Kingsville.

The Foxy Grandma
Governor Ann Richards was elected in 1990, but she had already become famous for her keynote address in the 1988 Democratic National Convention. She said of Vice President George H. W. Bush, "Poor George, he can't help it. He was born with a silver foot in his mouth." Richards had been state treasurer before she ran for governor against Clayton Williams, a candidate known for keeping one foot firmly in his mouth at

all times. Richards started the Texas Lottery, buying the first ticket in 1992 (it was not a winner). In an ironic twist of fate so common in Texas, she was defeated for her second term by George W. Bush, the son of President George H. W. Bush.

Vroom!

The magazine *Texas Monthly* had Richards on the cover in one of the most famous illustrations of the former governor. Dressed in white leather, Richards appears to be straddling a fully decked out Harley-Davidson motorcycle. In reality, her head was spliced onto the body of a model. Later she'd spoof the cover herself, showing up for an event on a black Harley-Davidson in black leather.

INFAMOUS MOMENTS
IN TEXAS POLITICS

Ballot Box 13
In Alice, Texas, several days after the runoff primary election
for U.S. senator in 1948 between Lyndon B. Johnson and Coke
Stevenson, an amended vote tally from Box 13 gave Johnson an
additional 202 votes. Stevenson got one additional vote. But
there was something odd about Johnson's new votes. They were
cast in alphabetical order, and the handwriting for all the signa-
tures was the same. Many of the "voters" were actually dead.
Despite all of this and an investigation by the Texas Rangers,
the votes were accepted as valid and Johnson was declared the
winner by 87 votes.

Vote Early, Vote Often

The dead in Texas have also signed Republican petitions seeking
to nominate three candidates: Pete du Pont, Bob Dole and
Alexander Haig. Political consultant Rocky Mountain (yes,
really) was convicted on 38 counts of forgery. His firm had
arranged a forgery party for teenagers with free beer and lists of
names to place on petitions.

Take This Gun and Shoot Me!
In 1981, Representative Mike Martin offered his cousin a
$30,000-per-year state job if he'd shoot him in the arm with
a shotgun. Martin wasn't suicidal, just ambitious. He was apparently trying to gain sympathy votes so he could win a race for
State Senate. He claimed to have been attacked by everyone
from a masked assailant to his opposition. In the meantime, his
cousin laid out the truth for the grand jury. Martin was indicted
for perjury and did not run for re-election.

Killer Bees! Run!

In Texas, a conversation about killer bees is not always about the insects. In May 1979, a dozen Democratic senators eluded everyone—from the Texas Rangers to the press—for five days to break quorum in the State Senate and kill a bill in the Legislature. The bill would have benefited the Republican presidential hopefuls, and the senators realized their only hope to kill the bill was to leave altogether. Nine hid out in an Austin apartment, one hid in Houston, one in Mexico and another in South Texas. They were called the "killer bees" because an opponent noted that you never knew where they'd hit next.

We'll Just Skip the Letter C...

The killer bee approach was repeated in 2003 when 52 Democrats, now the minority party, attempted to fight redistricting in the state by fleeing to Oklahoma (which apparently has no extradition treaty with Texas). Even the Department of Homeland Security was pulled into the search for the missing Democrats. No one found them until they turned up on CNN. Dubbed the "Killer Ds," the senators successfully prevented Republican passage of the redistricting plan during the 2003 regular session, although the measure passed in a later special session. Three years later, the U.S. Supreme Court found the controversial redistricting of one district in the plan was a violation of the Voting Rights Act.

It Was the Food

Agriculture Commissioner Reagan Brown lost a re-election bid in 1982 after he made a racial slur. He blamed it on food poisoning from a bad turkey sandwich. African-American legislator Craig Washington quipped that Brown was probably eating a "big redneck sandwich."

Boot-in-Mouth Disease

The most colorful boot-in-mouth disease candidate in Texas history was Clayton Williams. Known to both his friends and enemies as Claytie, he lost an election everyone was sure he'd win handily. Although he was an ideal Texas gubernatorial candidate—a rich, connected cowboy—the voters of Texas could not bring themselves to elect a candidate who compared rape to bad weather. His notorious rape quote: "If it's inevitable, just relax and enjoy it." Inexplicably, he followed up by acknowledging that he'd sought prostitutes in Mexico as a youth to get "serviced." Claytie spent $8 million of his own money on his campaign, bringing his total to nearly $22 million, while his opponent, Ann Richards, spent $14 million on her campaign. Richards won, becoming the first female governor to win in her own right.

Behind Every Great Man is a Great Woman—and Sometimes, Another Woman

Henry Cisneros was the first Hispanic mayor of a large American city: San Antonio. Charismatic and talented, he served four times as mayor and was eventually tapped to be Secretary of Housing and Urban Development. However his long time affair and subsequent efforts to hide money he'd paid his mistress forced him to leave office and derailed his political aspirations. Instead, he became president of Univision, a Spanish-language television network, the fifth largest in the U.S.

POLITICAL PARAPHERNALIA

Amen to That

Nowhere is prayer more needed than in Texas politics. And no one delivered better prayers than Dr. Gerald Mann. Mann was the official chaplain of the Texas Legislature from 1975 to 1995. He established a tradition of delivering one-line "zinger" prayers to open sessions of the Legislature. Here are some favorites:

☛ "Let us do what we must do now; there may be a law against it tomorrow."

☛ "Teach us the difference between an open mind and an empty head."

☛ "Remind us that America is a country of taxation which was founded to avoid taxation."

☛ "We are grateful that when Moses parted the Red Sea, he didn't have to write the Environmental Impact Statement."

☛ "We thank you that there's nothing wrong with the younger generation that becoming taxpayers won't cure."

☛ "May all of the wild oats we've sown experience crop failure."

☛ "Let us remember that women will never be the equal of men until they can be bald and still think they are good looking."

☛ "Remind us that the best foundations are built with the rocks people throw at us."

From a Distance, She Looks Pretty Good

During the restoration of the Capitol in Austin in the 1980s, one long-standing mystery was finally solved—the woman on the top of the Capitol building holding the Texas star is made of zinc. Known as the Goddess of Liberty, the Goddess of Texas or the Goddess of Wisdom, depending on who you ask, the woman was also found to be quite…well, ugly, truth be told. Her features were greatly exaggerated so she would look normal from down below. At least that's the theory. Interestingly enough, the statue atop the dome in Washington, DC, is quite lovely, even close up. Another discovery during the renovation was that the goddess' head once held a hive of bees, which had apparently flown in and out her nose.

After she had been sandblasted and repainted and was presumably bee-free, the goddess was returned to her renovated perch via a National Guard Sikorsky Skycrane helicopter. What was to take 20 minutes turned into a three-day ordeal, thanks to high winds in the area. How she got up there without a helicopter the first time is a mystery lost in the annals of Texas history. Perhaps she was raised on hot air.

Did He Just Say That?

Texas politicians excel in the realm of colorful quotes. Here are some of the more famous (and infamous).

"Ain't nothin' in the middle of the road but yellow stripes and dead armadillos."

–Agriculture Commissioner Jim Hightower

"And now, will y'all stand and be recognized?"

–House Speaker Gib Lewis to a group of handicapped people in wheelchairs (Lewis had an unprecedented gift for gaff)

"Oh good. Now he'll be bi-ignorant."

–Agriculture Commissioner Jim Hightower when told that Governor Bill Clements had been studying Spanish

"I'd just make a little bit of money, I wouldn't make a whole lot."

–House Speaker Gib Lewis, defending himself against the charge that he would personally profit from a bill he had introduced

"I am filled with humidity."

–Gib Lewis, again

"If it's dangerous to talk to yourself, it's probably even dicier to listen..."

–Agriculture Commissioner Jim Hightower

"I move we recess to go outside and throw up."

–House Speaker Gib Lewis during a budget hearing

"My friend, I can explain it to you, but I can't understand it for you."

–Comptroller John Sharp, addressing the legislature regarding a business tax plan

IF YOU'RE GOING TO DO THE CRIME...

The Wild, Wild West in 2005

In 2005, Texas ranked second in the country in terms of population, eighth in terms of total crime and 13th in terms of violent crime. Within Texas, the most dangerous city could be either Dallas or Houston, depending on how you look at the numbers. The safest city with a population of over a million is Austin; you might not even bother locking your car there.

Dallas
Murders: 202 (16.4 per 100,000 people)
Assaults: 7783 (632.6 per 100,000 people)
Auto thefts: 14,277 (1160.4 per 100,000 people)

Houston
Murders: 334 (16.3 per 100,000 people)
Assaults: 11653 (569.6 per 100,000 people)
Auto thefts: 20,408 (997.6 per 100,000 people)

Austin
Murders: 26 (3.8 per 100,000 people)
Assaults: 1873 (270.3 per 100,000 people)
Auto thefts: 2548 (367.7 per 100,000 people)

But Texas Can Catch 'Em

As of 2000, Texas had the nation's largest incarcerated population. Since 1990, nearly one in five new prisoners added to U.S. prisons called Texas their home behind bars. In fact, more Texans are under criminal justice control—in prison, in jail, on parole or on probation—than the *entire* population of Alaska. If Texas was a country, it would have the world's highest incarceration rate and the third biggest prison system. There are 117 state prisons, which doesn't include county prisons or the 11 federal institutions in the state. Some of the more interesting names are Roach Prison, Skyview Psychiatric and Mountain View (which houses female death-row inmates). There's even a Texas Prison Museum, complete with exhibits of prisoner contraband, inmate art and "Old Sparky," a decommissioned electric chair.

DID YOU  KNOW?

The Texas correctional system has grown so large that in July of 2000, corrections officials ran out of six-digit numbers to assign to inmates. They officially created prisoner number one million.

The Oldest Prison in Texas
The city of Huntsville is home to nine prisons, including the Walls Unit in Huntsville Prison, where the majority of Texas

executions take place. The most infamous event at Huntsville was the 1974 Carrasco prison siege. For 11 days starting on July 24, 1974, Federico Gomez Carrasco, a drug boss from South Texas, led a siege of the prison. Carrasco, who was serving life for assault with the intent to murder a police officer, used his connections to smuggle weapons and ammo into the prison. With the help of two other inmates, he took 11 workers and four other inmates hostage in the prison's library. He demanded bulletproof helmets and vests and planned on using the hostages as shields for his escape. Then one of the hostages suggested they create a moving structure made up of law books (which they thought would stop bullets) and chalkboards as a sort of escape pod. They secured eight hostages to the moving barricade and headed for an armored car. Prison officials blasted the structure with fire hoses, effectively illustrating the flaw in the plan. Carrasco ended up committing suicide, one of his accomplices was killed by officers, and two hostages were killed by the gang. The final accomplice was later executed.

DID YOU KNOW?

A man was once imprisoned in Huntsville because he was deemed worthless.

A Deadly State

Texas has executed more people than any other place in the Western world. No other state in the U.S. even comes close. Of all of the executions carried out in the U.S. between 1977 and 1998, one-third were carried out in Texas. The state executed 40 prisoners in 2000 alone. While the death chamber is in Huntsville, death row is not. Male inmates on death row spend their last days in the Polunsky Unit in Livingston, north of Houston. Female inmates are in Galveston in the Mountain View Unit.

At first, Texas used hanging for executions, then went with the electric chair starting in 1923. Prior to 1923, each county was responsible for its own executions, but the move to the electric chair centralized things. The last inmate to be electrocuted was Joseph Johnson in July 1964. The state moved to lethal injection as a method of execution until 1972, when the Supreme Court declared capital punishment "cruel and unusual punishment." Forty-five men on death row had their sentences changed to life in prison. The legislature adjusted the Penal Code to allow for the death penalty, but it took 10 years before the first person, Charlie Brooks, was executed under the law. As of March 2007, there were 377 men awaiting execution in Texas.

Three women have been executed in Texas since 1982. Karla Faye Tucker (executed in 1998) was the first woman executed since the Civil War. Betty Lou Beets (executed in 2000) killed her abusive husband and, at age 62, was the oldest person put to death in Texas. Frances Newton (executed in 2005) was convicted of killing her husband and two children, but she maintained her innocence up to the end. As of 2007, there were 10 women on death row.

DID YOU  KNOW?

The last statements of death row inmates executed since 1982 are maintained on the Texas Department of Criminal Justice website.

Texas Rangers: The Long Arm of the Law in Texas

Colonel Homer Garrison Jr., long-time director of the Texas Department of Public Safety, described the Texas Rangers as "men who could not be stampeded." The Rangers are the oldest state law enforcement agency in North America. Over the years, the Rangers have investigated political corruption and murder, acted as riot police and detectives and been a quasi-military force. Originally formed in 1823 by Stephen F. Austin to deal with Indian raids, Rangers had to provide their own arms, horses and equipment. Although they were promised pay, in those early years that promise was rarely kept.

Rangers came from all the varied cultural backgrounds of the state—Mexican, Anglo and even Native American. They borrowed equipment from one another and often carried multiple weapons because they were so often outnumbered. One writer noted that a Texas Ranger could "ride like a Mexican, trail like an Indian, shoot like a Tennessean, and fight like the devil." It was a group of Texas Rangers who were the only men to ride in response to Colonel William B. Travis' last-minute plea to defend the Alamo. They died fighting.

The Texas Rangers still investigate major felonies, although other law enforcement agencies tend to handle gambling- and drug-related crimes. There are 116 Texas Rangers, and each one is responsible for two to three counties. They are not issued uniforms, but they are issued a badge and all equipment.

Wanted: Dead, Not Alive

In the 1930s, bank robberies were rampant, and the Texas Bankers Association offered a standing $5000 reward for bank robbers. There was just one condition. The robber had to be dead. This led to a series of phony hold-ups where criminals would hire someone to rob a bank, shoot him and then collect the reward. A Texas Ranger, Captain Frank H. Hamer, went to the press and explained what was happening. The bankers changed their policy.

Finding Bonnie and Clyde

It was the same Captain Hamer who put an end to the work of Bonnie and Clyde. He left the Rangers when Ma Ferguson became governor, but the superintendent of the Texas prison system asked him to track down Clyde Barrow and Bonnie Parker. Hamer agreed, taking a brief commission as a Texas highway patrolman. He trailed the couple for 102 days and, with other officers including another former Ranger, caught up with them in Louisiana. They had hoped to capture Bonnie and Clyde alive, but ended up firing 130 rounds into the couple instead.

MOVIES

Get Discovered in Texas

Texas, in addition to having many miles of filmable landscape, has 15 permanent sets. Ranging from western towns to battle-ships, they are all listed on the Texas Film Commission's web-site. The USS *Lexington* is noted for being film friendly and accessible—yet it can appear, from the right angle, to be miles offshore. Some sets do double duty. The Indian Cliffs Ranch around El Paso has an 1850s replica of a frontier fort and a slightly more modern war set including helicopters, tanks and army trucks. Dallas is home to a Middle Eastern set designed to simulate An Nasiriyah in Iraq for a television movie about the rescue of U.S. soldier Private Jessica Lynch. However, the film commission notes that the set could easily be adapted for an Old Mexico look.

DID YOU KNOW?

The events behind the infamous 1974 movie *The Texas Chainsaw Massacre* did not actually happen in Texas. The movie was loosely based on the story of Ed Gein from Wisconsin. Gein did not use a chainsaw in his crimes; in 1957 he shot both of his victims. He did, however, skin his victims. Gein was also the twisted inspiration for both *Psycho* and *The Silence of the Lambs*.

Where the Stars Touch the Ground

More than 1300 "projects" (to use the Hollywood lingo) have been made in Texas since 1910. Here are a few notables shot in the Lone Star State:

Wings: Filmed in 1927, this silent movie about World War I fighter pilots was the first film to win the Academy Award for best picture. It also featured a male-on-male kiss—strictly fraternal. *Wings* was filmed in San Antonio and starred Clara Bow, Charles "Buddy" Rogers and Richard Arlen. Gary Cooper was in the movie as well. Rogers didn't know how to fly a plane when filming began, but he learned how to do so by the end of it. It was also a real war movie: thousands of extras battled on the ground, dozens of planes flew overhead and explosions went off everywhere. Miraculously, only two accidents occurred. In one mishap, stunt pilot Dick Grace was injured while performing a planned plane crash. The other was a fatal accident. An army pilot helping out crashed his plane and was killed. The investigation held that the pilot, not the director, was responsible for the accident, and filming went on.

Giant: Aptly named, this 1956 epic starred the biggest stars of its time: Elizabeth Taylor, Rock Hudson and James Dean. It's known for half a dozen reasons, not the least being that at the time, it was the most expensive movie ever made. It was the top moneymaker for Warner Brothers until *Superman* came along in 1978. *Giant* is also remembered for a tragedy. James Dean, who played the quiet cowhand, died in an automobile accident late in the filming, and another actor had to provide a voice-over for a few of his lines. Dean was nominated posthumously for an Oscar. *Giant* was filmed on location in Marfa.

DID YOU KNOW?

In *Giant*, there is a massive painting in the home. It now hangs in the Menger Hotel in San Antonio.

The Alamo: This movie was the pinnacle of a thousand westerns. Starring John Wayne as Colonel Davy Crockett and, oddly enough, Frankie Avalon as "Smitty," the 1960 epic of the single most famous battle in Texas history was filmed on a set outside of Brackettville that took two years to build. After filming, the set fell into disrepair and was torn down in 1985 to be rebuilt to proper scale in 1988 for another Alamo movie (*Alamo: The Price of Freedom*). The rebuilt set was used again for two other movies, *Lonesome Dove* and *Bad Girls*. John Wayne would return to Texas in 1968 to star in *Hellfighters*, a film shot in Houston about oil well firefighter Red Adair.

Bonnie and Clyde: Shot in Dallas (no pun intended), Warren Beatty and Faye Dunaway starred as the infamous bank robbers who were hunted down by former Texas Ranger Frank Hamer, played by Denver Pyle. It was the screen debut for Gene Wilder, who played the funeral director Eugene Grizzard. Warner Brothers didn't think the film would do very well, so they offered Beatty 40 percent of the gross instead of the more common minimal fee for a first-time producer. The movie went on to gross over $50 million.

Benji: Starring Higgins, a scruffy mutt with a gift for mugging for the camera, *Benji* was shot in McKinney. Higgins did all his own doggy stunts at the ripe old age of 14. That's 69 in dog years. Higgins was an old hand in show business; he'd worked on the TV series *Petticoat Junction*. The ultimate underdog, *Benji* proved its worth. The film became the fifth highest grossing film of 1974 and led to numerous sequels.

Robocop: Although the story is set in Detroit, the film was shot in Dallas. The entrance to the Omni Consumer Products (OCP) building (the privatized police force) in the movie is actually the entrance of Dallas City Hall, with matte work drawn in the film to make the building appear to be a giant skyscraper. This is despite the fact that Dallas has plenty of available skyscrapers. Other Dallas cityscapes in the film include the Plaza of the Americas and the Fountain Place building. The *Robocop* sequel was also filmed in Dallas.

DID YOU  KNOW?

The Robocop costume was so hot that an air conditioner had to be installed in it.

Spy Kids: Texas native Robert Rodriguez has directed a number of his movies in the state, including the *Spy Kids* movies, *Sin City* and *The Adventures of Sharkboy and Lavagirl*. He doesn't merely use the state as a location, though. He has broken the mold and actually edits his movies in his garage in Austin. But don't look for oil stains on his floor. The garage is a state-of-the-art editing studio so sophisticated that Rodriguez convinced Quentin Tarantino to go from shooting on film to shooting digitally.

DID YOU  KNOW?

After California and New York, Texas ranks third in the country when it comes to money spent by the film industry. In 2004 alone, the industry brought in more than $150 million in revenue to the state. Since then, however, financial incentives from other states have drawn some of that business away from Texas.

MADE FOR TV

Big Hits on the Little Screen

Texas has never snubbed the little screen. Several television series have been shot in the state, as well as countless music videos and made-for-TV movies. Here are a few of the runaway hits on the little screen.

Dallas: One of the most successful drama series on television was *Dallas*, based on a fabulously wealthy but hopelessly dysfunctional Texas oil family, the Ewings. The main villain, J.R. Ewing, played by Fort Worth's own Larry Hagman, became the man America loved to hate. Interestingly enough, J.R. was originally designed as a supporting character. He quickly took over the limelight, and the series soon revolved around his dirty deals.

Barney: It's shouldn't come as a surprise that Barney is from Texas, given his size, but since he doesn't have a trace of an accent, most people wonder if he's a transplant from up north. This six-foot purple dinosaur is as native as a longhorn. He started out as a home video project of two former teachers in Dallas, making the leap to PBS after a network executive's child fell in love with Barney after watching the video. Now an international star and preschool sensation, *Barney* has moved beyond PBS with a line of toys, videos and music. *Barney's Favorites: Volume 1*, the big dinosaur's first CD, has gone triple platinum.

Walker, Texas Ranger: Texas does like its good guys, too. Chuck Norris, martial artist and actor, went western as Cordell Walker, Texas Ranger. The series ran for eight seasons and was filmed in Dallas, where locals were frequently used as extras. A signature move on *Walker, Texas Ranger* was a roundhouse kick to the head, often repeated in slow motion and from multiple angles, karate movie–style.

THEATER

Is This Seat Taken?

Houston has a bustling Theater District. The district spans 17 blocks and is second only to New York in the number of theater seats in a downtown area. There are 12,948 seats for live performances and 1480 for movies. More than two million people visit the Theater District every year. In Houston, visitors can enjoy a performance by any one of a number of permanent professional resident companies, including the Alley Theater, the Houston Grand Opera (which has won a Grammy, a Tony and an Emmy), the Houston Ballet and the Houston Symphony.

The Gus S. Wortham Center is the home to the Houston Ballet and the Houston Grand Opera. It opened in 1987 (under budget and four months early) and is so immense that you could fit a six-story building into the foyer and three football fields on the roof. Even more incredible, the Wortham Center was funded entirely by private contributions, in the amount of $66 million. Inside, there are two theaters: the Alice and George Brown Theater and the Roy and Lillie Cullen Theater. The Brown, which is the larger theater, seats 2423 and has a 17,000-square-foot stage. It also has more than three-quarters of a mile of catwalks and walkways overhead.

MUSIC

Let's Go Out and Hear Some Music

Austin is self-proclaimed as the "Live Music Capital of the World." Get off the airplane in Austin and you're likely to hear a local band performing on a stage set for live performances. The nexus of live, original music in Austin revolves around 6th Street, where, on any given weekend, people gather to hear the next Stevie Ray Vaughn or Lucinda Williams. With more live music venues per capita than any other city in the country, it's little wonder that the city is host to one of the music industry's key conferences: SXSW.

The Musician's Music Festival

South by Southwest, known by its initials SXSW, is one of the country's largest music festivals. Held every spring in Austin, it's much more than a festival. It's a conference for the music industry, attracting hundreds and hundreds of recording industry professionals, an equal number of musicians and thousands of fans. There are 64 official venues during the week-long event, along with countless unofficial venues. Bands from across the country come to SXSW in hopes of being discovered, while industry veterans come looking for the next big thing (and to do a little networking). SXSW is not just about listening to music, though. The focus is on music as an industry. At its heart, it's a trade show, complete with exhibits and industry-specific panel presentations. In 2007, according to the event brochure, attendees can learn about "Touring on a Shoestring Budget" or discover "China's Emerging Music Market." Others might get more out of "A Field Guide to Indie Labels," while blows might be exchanged during the panel discussion entitled, "Why Does Today's Music Sound Like Shit?" So who gives the keynote address at SXSW? In 2007, it's Pete Townsend from the Who.

FAMOUS TEXANS

Nearly Texan

Several famous people are so identified with the state that they should have been from Texas. But, as a bumper sticker seen around the state says, "I'm not from Texas, but I got here as soon as I could."

☞ Both President George Herbert Walker Bush (often referred to as "Senior") and President George Walker Bush were born in New England, the former in Massachusetts and the latter in Connecticut. But Senior's presidential library is in Texas, and, at this writing, Junior's is likely to be.

☞ Cowboy actors John Wayne and Slim Pickens were born in Iowa and California, respectively.

☞ Roger Staubach, beloved quarterback for the Dallas Cowboys during their reign as Super Bowl champions, was born in Ohio.

☞ Jerry Jeff Walker, a famed Texas musician, was born in New York.

☞ Stephen F. Austin, considered the father of Texas, was born in Virginia.

☞ Molly Ivans, journalist and best-selling author, was born in California.

Native Sons and Daughters

Still, Texas has its share of native-born stars:

- George Foreman: born in Marshall, went on to boxing and grilling fame

- Willie Nelson: born in Abbott, musician, avid runner and Texas icon

- Lyle Lovett: born in Klein, former Aggie and singer-songwriter

- Carol Burnett: born in San Antonio, comedian and actress

- Sam Donaldson: born in El Paso, news anchor and broadcast journalist

- Larry McMurtry: born in Wichita, Falls novelist best known for *Lonesome Dove*

- Tommy Lee Jones: born in San Saba, actor

- Robert Rodriguez: born in San Antonio, film director, producer and screenwriter

HIGH SCHOOL FOOTBALL

Picking Sides

The rivalries in Texas between educational institutions are legendary, all stemming from the state religion: football.

The modern day era of Texas school football began in 1951 when the University Interscholastic League (UIL is the organizing body of school competitions of every sort in Texas and the largest interschool organization in the world) established a plan that provided rankings based on school enrollment. The largest schools would be considered 4A, the smallest Class B. The system changed to 5A through 1A in the 1980s, then 5A division I and 5A division II in the 1990s. Powerhouse teams emerged from the plains of Texas, including Abilene's Cooper Cougars, Midland's Robert E. Lee Bulldogs (the "dawgs" won three consecutive state titles, 1998–2000) and most famously, Odessa's Permian Basin Panthers.

You Were So Famous...In High School

There was even a Texas High School Football Hall of Fame, which eventually became part of the Texas High School Sports Hall of Fame in Waco. In 2006, the Texas grocery chain H-E-B (named for Charles E. Butt, but that's another story) produced a book—*The Greatest Moments in Texas High School Football History*—for the playoff games held in San Antonio's Alamodome.

Friday Night Lights Are On!

The Odessa Permian Panthers have won six state championships, played in three other title games and ranked twice as unofficial national champions. The team's 1988 run to the state championship was the subject of the film *Friday Night Lights*,

a movie that provides a brief glimpse into the community's complete obsession with the team. The Panthers play in Ratliff Stadium, known as the "epicenter of Texas high school football." The stadium is wired for television, and games are rebroadcast locally, with playoff games often broadcast live. It cost $5.6 million to build in 1982, seats 19,302 fans and has been named one of the top 10 high school football stadiums in the U.S. by *USA Today*. Many Permian grads go on to play at major universities but often bemoan the small crowds and comparatively modest coaching programs.

The Sugar Land Express

Kenneth Hall is a legend in Texas high school football. Known as the "Sugar Land Express," Hall's career rushing record of 11,232 yards still stands as the national record over 50 years later, along with four other national records. Only Emmitt Smith, who was in Florida at the time and would eventually become a Dallas Cowboy, topped Hall's record of 33 100-yard games. Hall was a quarterback and running back for Sugarland High and went on to play for Texas A&M and the Houston Oilers, though he was never the stunning success he was in high school. The Kenneth Hall Trophy, which features his likeness, is presented annually to the most outstanding high school player in the country.

PRO FOOTBALL

America's Team Lives in Texas

They call themselves "America's Team," but technically they belong to Texas, through and through. The Dallas Cowboys are more than a football team; they are an icon in a state full of icons. The blue and white uniforms, the outlined star and the silver helmets are as recognizable as the state flag. *Forbes* magazine lists the Cowboys as one of the most valuable sports teams in North America, with an estimated value of $1.17 billion. The team generates almost $250 million in annual revenue. The Cowboys hold the NFL's record for the most consecutive winning seasons (20), the most postseason appearances (28), the most NFC Championship games (14) and the most Super Bowl appearances (8).

Good Guys Wear White

The Cowboys started the tradition of wearing their white jerseys at home games. It used to be that most teams wore their colored jerseys at home, but now under NFL rules, the home team picks which color their team will wear. Because most teams will wear their colored jersey at home, the Cowboys are most often seen playing, both in home and away games, in white.

Hall of Fame Tiff

The Cowboys are not, according to most avid fans, well represented in the Pro Football Hall of Fame. This perceived injustice causes considerable consternation to the faithful. Some people imply it's because the team is relatively young, having been founded in 1960, while teams with greater representation in the Hall of Fame were founded in 1933 or before. The debate continues to rage. Although the Cowboys are tied with the 49ers and the Steelers for the most Super Bowl wins (five), Dallas holds the record for the most Super Bowl MVPs (seven).

The only time a Super Bowl MVP came from the losing team (and the first time a defensive player was chosen) was when Cowboy linebacker Chuck Howley was selected in 1971 in the game against the Colts.

The Cowboys do not retire jersey numbers. Instead, they have a Ring of Honor, which is on permanent display and encircles the field at Texas Stadium. Seventeen Cowboy players, a head coach and a general manager are on the ring. It includes Tory Aikman, Emmitt Smith and Michael Irvin, known collectively as the Triplets.

 Roger Staubach (known as Captain Comeback) threw the first and most famous Hail Mary pass in history in the NFC Divisional Playoff game in 1975. He threw a desperate 50-yard winning touchdown pass to Drew Pearson to defeat the Vikings. Staubach, a Catholic, said he "closed his eyes and said a Hail Mary." He may not have invented the long pass, but he certainly named it.

Rah! Rah! Rah!

The Dallas Cowboys Cheerleaders are nearly as famous as the Cowboys themselves and are arguably the most well-known set of cheerleaders in the world. They started out as the Cowbelles & Beaux, formed from local high school students. In the 1970s, they got a boost when Cowboys manager Tex Schramm decided to change their image to increase attendance. He tried a quick fix by hiring professional models at first, but they weren't up for the athletic end of cheerleading, so he developed a new squad that combined looks with athletic ability and knack for performance. By 1979, there was a Dallas Cheerleader made-for-TV movie starring Jane Seymour, and members of the team have made cameo appearances on a wide variety of TV shows and specials, including *Wife Swap*.

DID YOU  KNOW?

The median pay for a player on the Dallas Cowboys is $384,840 per season as of 2005. A Cowboys cheerleader makes $15 per game. Guess who's buying dinner?

She's Not From Around Here, but Let's Give Her a Try
There is no residency requirement to be one of America's favorite cheerleaders. A Miss New York has been a Dallas Cowboys Cheerleader.

Nice Pom-Poms

The porn classic *Debbie Does Dallas* focuses on a team of cheerleaders attempting to raise money to try out for a team that is a spoof of the Dallas Cowboys Cheerleaders. No one "does" anyone in Dallas, ironically. There were five sequels and numerous spin-offs involving Debbie "doing" several other cities.

Oilers Tap Out

Houston was home to the Houston Oilers, a charter member of the American Football League, for 36 years. They were the first professional football team to play in a domed stadium, the Houston Astrodome, in 1968. The Oilers won one conference championship and eight division championships, but they never made it into the Super Bowl. After the city refused to deliver a new stadium, owner Bud Adams moved the team to Nashville in 1998. They are now the Tennessee Titans, but Adams retained the right to the name Oilers. Famous Oilers include Warren Moon, Earl Campbell and Jim Norton. Houston finally made its way back into the NFL in 2002 with an expansion team, the Houston Texans. The Texans play in the new Reliant Stadium (named for a local energy company, Reliant Energy), which features the NFL's first retractable roof.

BASKETBALL

If You Prefer Your Balls Round...

It's not all about football in Texas. There is a bit of basketball in the state. Texas is home to the beloved San Antonio Spurs (the only major professional sports franchise in the city), the Dallas Mavericks and the Houston Rockets.

Even the Fans are Bigger in Texas

The San Antonio Spurs fans have set several NBA attendance records, including the largest crowd ever for an NBA finals game (1999), and are considered among the most loyal fans in the NBA. The Spurs were originally a Dallas team, the Dallas Chaparrals, but were put up for sale after missing the playoffs for the first time in 1972–73. The San Antonio Spurs have won three national championships and have been referred to as choirboys by their own coach for their relatively calm demeanor.

BASEBALL

Trading in Revolvers for Ray Guns

The Houston Astros started out as part of the third league in baseball, the Continental League. While the league itself never got anywhere, it did bring major league baseball to other markets—in this case, Houston. The team, originally named the Houston Colt .45s, took the field in 1962. Then, in late 1964, they moved into the Astrodome and a few months later changed their name to the Astros, to the significant relief of the Colt Firearms Company, which disliked the infringement on its company name. The new name seemed more futuristic, which was fitting, given NASA had based its astronaut training program in Houston. Even the groundskeepers wore mock spacesuits in keeping with the theme.

The Domed Stadium

The Astrodome itself was dubbed the "Eighth Wonder of the World." Its domed roof allowed for cool play even in the brutal heat and humidity of a Houston summer. Despite significant engineering challenges, including flattening the roof and using a new paving process to deal with soil issues, the Astrodome was completed six months ahead of schedule. The roof, which was originally transparent Lucite, was painted black because the players kept losing the fly balls in the glare. This caused the grass to die, and for a year the Astros played on green-painted dirt and dead grass. Monsanto, which had created Astroturf for homeowners, came to the rescue the next season, although they only had enough artificial turf on hand for the infield. Three months later they finished the outfield, leaving dirt around the bases.

Astrodome Miscellanea

One of the largest crowds in the Astrodome's history wasn't there for a sporting event. They were there to see Tejano superstar Selena in 1995. More than 64,000 fans were on hand for what would be Selena's last concert—she was murdered later that year. WrestleMania broke Selena's record in 2001 with 67,925 fans.

Here are some more Astrodome facts:

- ☛ At a height of 218-feet, the Astrodome could house an 18-story building.

- ☛ The playing field is actually 25 feet below street level.

- ☛ It cost $35 million to build in 1965 and $60 million to expand in 1989.

- ☛ The doors to the superstadium were opened for non-entertainment purposes in 2005 when it was used as a temporary home for Hurricane Katrina survivors.

Tragedy on the Mound

In January of 1975, former Astros pitcher Don Wilson committed suicide. Wilson had pitched two no-hitters for the Astros—he struck out Hank Aaron for the final out in 1967, and in 1969, Wilson struck out 235 batters. He was 29 years old when he committed suicide by leaving his car running in his garage. Tragically, though he tried to seal off the garage, the fumes rose into his home and took the life of his five-year-old son as well.

And Rounding the Bases for the Millionth Time...
The millionth run in Major League Baseball was scored by Astro Bob Watson on May 4, 1975. Because other players in other stadiums were also playing that night, Watson had to run at full speed to ensure he'd be the one credited with the historic run.

Guess Who They Hired for General Manager?

In 1994, the Astros hired the first African-American general manager in Major League Baseball: Bob Watson, the man with the millionth run. Watson was only with the team for one year; he left the Astros after the 1995 season to become general manager of the New York Yankees. He ended up leading the Yankees to a World Championship in 1996, their first championship since 1978.

The Big Dance

The Astros finally made it to the World Series in 2005. In fact, on October 25, 2005, the Astros hosted the first World Series game ever played in Texas. The team, which by this time had moved out of the Astrodome, played the Chicago White Sox in Minute Maid Park in Houston (Minute Maid Park was briefly named Enron Field, but was renamed after Enron went bankrupt). They were swept in the series but managed in Game 3 to play the longest game in the history of the World Series. It went 14 innings.

Staying in the Game

The Astros had two other longest games. On October 15, 1986, Game 6 of the 1986 National League Championship Series against the New York Mets went 16 innings; Houston lost 6–7. On October 9, 2005, Game 4 of the 2005 National League Division Series against the Atlanta Braves went 18 innings; Houston won 7–6.

The Rangers

The Texas Rangers came to Arlington in 1972 with Ted Williams as their manager. He retired the next season, and it wasn't until 1995 that things looked up for the Rangers. That year they made it to the playoffs, eventually losing to the New York Yankees. The Rangers have won three West Division titles but have never made it any further. The team was once owned by President George W. Bush.

The Arm That Wouldn't Stop

Nolan Ryan played with the Astros in 1980, agreeing to the first
million-dollar-per-year salary. That was the year the Astros were
stopped one game short of the World Series. During his time
with the Astros, Ryan became the all-time strikeout leader. He
left the team in 1989 to head north—to Dallas and the Texas
Rangers—after being considered "too old" by Astros owner
John McMullen (Ryan was 40; McMullen was 71). Ryan went
on to pitch two more no-hitters with the Rangers and entered
the Hall of Fame as a Texas Ranger. The Astros are the only
team to have had Nolan Ryan, Roger Clemens and Randy
Johnson (the top three on the all-time strikeouts list) on their
roster at one point.

Ryan and Sosa

Despite not winning any of the big games, the Rangers have
had several notable players, mainly Nolan Ryan and Sammy
Sosa. Nolan Ryan is practically a Texas icon. He joined the
team when he was already in his 40s. Known as "the Ryan
Express," the pitcher played in a record-tying 27 seasons. His
pitches were regularly clocked at over 100 mph, even when he
was over 40 years old. He holds the record for the number of

no-hitters with seven (three more than any one else). He now owns two minor league teams in Texas—the Corpus Christi Hooks and the Round Rock Express.

When Sammy Sosa played baseball as a kid, he used a ball made out of tightly tied towels. This apparently taught him to hit just about anything, and he signed up with the Texas Rangers when he was 16, the youngest any player is allowed to sign a contract. He was traded away before he emerged as one of Major League Baseball's greatest power hitters, hitting a record 66 homeruns in 1998, just behind Mark McGuire's 70 homeruns the same season. President Bush has joked that trading Sammy Sosa was one of his worst decisions during his ownership of the team. Considered by most as the worst trade in baseball history, the Rangers traded Sosa and another rookie, Wilson Alvarez, to Chicago for Harold Baines. Sosa had been a Ranger for 43 days.

The Puffy Taco

Minor league baseball is big in Texas, and no other mascot in the state is as beloved, or as bizarre, as the San Antonio Missions' Henry the Puffy Taco. Actually, the Puffy Taco is the mascot of a local restaurant, Henry's Puffy Tacos. It all started when the restaurant wanted to advertise at the nearby stadium. What better way to catch people's attention than with a walking taco? During the seventh inning stretch, the Puffy Taco's main job is to race around the bases with a child chosen from the crowd. The young fan has to beat the taco to home plate to win a free dinner for the family. But it's not just a race. It's a take down—or should we say "take out"? The tradition is for the kid to actually tackle the Puffy Taco between third base and home plate, at which point the crowd goes wild and the child is heralded as a champion. The Texas State Legislature, which loves a good taco as much as the next guy, honored Henry the Puffy Taco in 2003 with House Resolution 490, recognizing him as "truly entertaining, hopelessly endearing and curiously appetizing." The Puffy Taco was named "Best Mascot in the Minor Leagues" by *Newsweek* magazine.

RODEO

Where There Are Cowboys, There's Rodeo

The call of a real cowboy is enough to push even championship teams out of their arenas. Rodeo is so big in Texas that two major sports franchises split their facility with the annual rodeo. In San Antonio, both the basketball and hockey teams have to hit the road and play away games during the rodeo.

You Might Want to Say "Hola" Instead of "Howdy"

Many of the events of the modern rodeo are based on the work of the *vaqueros* of Mexico. Vaqueros were the first cowboys of the American West, having worked with cattle for over 200 years before the first cattle drive. The word *vaquero* is a combination of the Spanish words for "cow" and "man." Vaqueros note that in Spanish they are called cow*men*, but in English they are demoted to cow*boys*. Now there's a macho interpretation.

Many words associated with cowboys are from Spanish:

- ☞ chaps: from the Spanish word *chaparreras*; leather leggings used to protect legs from brush and cactus.

- ☞ lasso: from the Spanish word *lazo*.

- ☞ rodeo: from the Spanish word *rodear*, which means "to encircle a herd."

- ☞ vamoose: from the Spanish word *vamos*, which means "let's go!"

- ☞ ranch: from the Spanish word *rancho*, which means, you guessed it, "ranch."

With 1.8 million people attending, the Houston Livestock Show and Rodeo is one big celebration. The livestock show is the largest in the world, with 27,068 entries. A single lamb was once sold for $104,000, and a grand champion steer went for $600,001! Those will be some pricey burgers. The rodeo garners over a million attendees and claims to be the world's largest. But if it is, it's not by much. Both the San Antonio and Fort Worth stock shows and rodeos claim over a million attendees as well. Houston, however, takes the prize for the most volunteers. It has 18,000 volunteers serving on 90 show committees.

Not Just Prize Livestock

The stock shows and rodeos are organized to provide scholarships, and between the San Antonio and Houston rodeos, they have given out a cumulative $271 million dollars in scholarships, grants and other prizes.

San Antonio Stats

San Antonio keeps some interesting stats on its annual rodeo. In 2007, over 4800 pounds of beef brisket were sold, along with 5000 foot-long hot dogs, most of which were probably washed down with 6405 gallons of soda. In the livestock section of the show, there were nearly two million pounds of beef on the hoof and over 990,000 pounds of pork. The horses kept busy drinking more than 50,000 gallons of water.

There's a Rodeo for Everyone

Big rodeos take place in every major city, and there are rodeos every weekend in Fort Worth. Smaller rodeos take place all over the state, including in towns such as Mesquite, Bulverde, Liberty Hill, Bandera and Jarrel. There's also an association for every kind of rodeo, including the Texas High School Rodeo Association, the Texas Amateur Rodeo Association, keeping rodeo a family tradition, and the Texas Gay Rodeo association, which has donated over $2 million to charity.

Rodeos have two types of events: roughstock and timed. In roughstock (bareback riding, saddle bronc riding and bull riding), the rider has to stay on for eight seconds, and both the bucker and buckee (horse and rider, respectively) are rated for showmanship. In timed events (barrel racing, roping, and wrestling), it's all about beating the clock.

No Wonder There Are So Many Big Buckles

Rodeo pros compete for, among other things, large belt buckles. Not surprisingly, the bigger the belt buckle, the better. It may be a badge of courage, a trophy or, in some cases, an inheritance, but as the years go on and the bucks stop bucking, it's just something that has to be loosened with great regularity.

Four Hundred Years of Tradition

Rodeos, like cowboys, come from a 400-year-old Mexican tradition—the *charreada*. Several charreada events still exist in rodeo in some form, but there are notable differences. The charreada focuses on horsemanship, and the arena is shaped like a keyhole. The *cala de caballo*, or "horse reining," involves a *charro*, or "cowboy," galloping his horse the length of the arena, sliding to a stop, pivoting the horse on each hind leg, performing several turns and then backing the horse to the starting point. A form of this event is a sport recognized by the American Quarter Horse Association. In *el paso de la muerte*, or "the pass of death," a charro riding bareback, with reins, must leap from his horse to a wild horse without reins and try to ride it until it stops bucking. Women have a special event as well. The *escaramuza*, or "skirmish," is a team of 8–12 women riding sidesaddle in precise patterns, barely missing each other as they make intertwining circles. One other difference—no one is paid for competing in a charreada. It's an honor to take part.

FAMOUS FEATS, RECORD BREAKERS AND OTHER FIRSTS

Flying High?

Move aside Orville and Wilbur Wright. While many may debate the claim, German immigrant Jacob Friedrich Brodbeck has gone into the annals of Texas history as the first man to fly an airplane. After grappling with an idea for more than 20 years, the pioneer school supervisor reportedly built a model "air-ship" in 1863 and introduced his idea at annual fairs and other community events. The response he received was positive enough to encourage a move to the next step—a full-sized version. And on September 20, 1865 (some sources date his first flight a few years later in 1868), his new and improved air-ship took to the skies. His efforts garnered him a quick flight, but fly he apparently did. The air-ship was said to have made it to an elevation of about 12 feet and soared for about 100 feet before plummeting back to earth. Brodbeck survived the ordeal with relatively few injuries. His invention, on the other hand, was totaled, and his investors were leery to put up the money for a second attempt. Legend has it that Brodbeck traveled the country in the hope of raising money, only to lose his original drawings and blueprints and all evidence that this story was indeed true. He died in 1910, just six years after the Wright brothers' successful first flight.

Another First

A more recent invention has the paperwork required to authenticate its claim as the first of its kind. And when you're in a pinch for cash and the banks are closed, chances are you've thanked your lucky stars for this particular modern convenience. Don Wetzel, an employee with the Dallas-based company Docutel, was the mind behind the ATM machine. The story goes that

the idea came to Wetzel in 1968 while waiting in a bank lineup. Five years and $5 million later, the Automated Teller Machine (ATM) as we know it made its first appearance. Of course, as with all inventions, an earlier claim to fame exists. Luther George Simjian, a Turkish immigrant to Florida, patented the idea in 1939 but was unable to convince banks of its potential usefulness.

That's My Invention!

Athens Café owner Fletcher Davis claimed to be the first to invent the hamburger sandwich back in the 1880s. According to published reports, however, he's not the only one. Others claiming the feat include Ohio brothers Frank and Charles Menches, whose claim dates back to 1885; Wisconsin native Charlie "Hamburger" Nagreen, who claimed to serve the first hamburger at the Outgamie County Fair in Seymor in 1885; and Louis Lassen of New Haven, Connecticut, who said he served the modern delicacy at his food stand in 1900. However, in each case bread was used instead of a bun. And the addition of cheese brings on another list of claims. Hmmmm.

For Your Convenience

Rare is the North American who hasn't stepped through the doors of a 7-Eleven. More rare still is the person who hasn't experienced a convenience store at all. Yet I'd be willing to bet that few individuals have a clue how the convenience store phenomenon developed. It seems Dallas can claim that invention, after the Southland Ice Co. began selling milk, eggs, and bread at its retail stores in 1927. The company soon called their outlets 7-Eleven—an easy reminder to patrons of its hours of operation—and later changed its name to 7-Eleven Inc. in 1999. Today there are more than 30,000 stores worldwide.

Spicy Soda

The oldest Dr. Pepper bottling plant was founded in 1891 in Dublin, Texas. It's also the only Dr. Pepper plant that still uses the original formula.

Snicker-Happy

Residents of Waco can't help but have a sweet tooth. The M&M/Mars plant in that city produces three-quarters of the world's Snickers bars.

Woolly State

In 2004, Texas produced more wool than any other state— 5.6 million pounds worth, in fact. Tom Green County calls itself the "Sheep and Wool Capital."

Tiny Tribute

While it's not known if it's the smallest flag in the world, students at the University of Texas at Dallas must have broken some kind of record when they replicated the American flag—50 stars, 13 stripes and all the red, white and blue you need—in miniscule form. The flag is so small you'd need to line up 10 of them, side by side, before its collective width would be as wide as a single strand of hair. The authors of this feat are Jang-Bae Jeon and Carlo Foresca.

Rare Beauties

The pink and purple pearls of Concho River mussels, found along the banks of the Concho River near San Angelo, are among the world's most rare pearls.

 The Tyler Municipal Rose Garden in Tyler first opened to the public in 1952. Covering 14 acres and made up of 40,000 rose bushes, the garden is considered the largest of its kind in the country.

Water, Water, Everywhere

In June 2000, San Angelo was granted the world record for the biggest water balloon fight in history. Almost 400 children gathered to toss 4400 water balloons to secure a spot in the *Guinness Book of World Records*. Sadly, since then, the record has been absolutely shattered. On April 23, 2006, almost 3000 Aussies tossed more than 55,000 water balloons at each other.

Literary Firsts

Victoria is home to the state's oldest women's literary club. Founded in 1855 by Viola Case, the Bronte Club began as a club for her students at the Victoria Female Academy. The venture began with a modest 11-volume collection of books, which were circulated among the students weekly. Over the years the club evolved into the Bronte Library, and is now the Victoria Public Library.

First of a Kind

Harlingen's Rachel McLish earned the first Ms. Olympia title at the inaugural U.S. Bodybuilding Championship in 1980. McLish won again in 1982, and over a relatively short four-year bodybuilding career, she managed four first-place finishes, three seconds and one third—a collection of accomplishments that eventually landed her in the Joe Weider's Bodybuilding Hall of Fame in 1999.

One Big Mouth

Augie, a Dallas family's pet golden retriever, made headlines on July 6, 2003, when he allowed someone to stuff five regulation-size tennis balls into his mouth. His reward for being such a good sport was a spot in the *Guinness Book of World Records* and a stint on *The Late Show* with David Letterman.

Rubik's Mania

Gonzales is the proud home of Casey Pernsteiner. In 2006, the 14-year-old young lady blew away her competition by consistently solving the Rubik's Cube puzzle with an average time of 14.62 seconds at the 2006 U.S. Nationals.

Record-Breaking Race

Ovalo is home to the youngest Grand American Rolex Sports Car Series winner in history. Colin Braun earned the title at the Daytona International Speedway in June 2006. He was exactly 17 years, 9 months and 7 days old at the time.

Ever the Maverick

Back in the 1850s, Texas rancher Sam Maverick apparently didn't like the idea of inflicting a hot iron brand on his cattle. His herd of unbranded cattle, which roamed about freely, was eventually termed "maverick." And over the years, the name has evolved to refer to an individual who takes an independent stand in life or "refuses to be branded." Maverick County is named in his honor.

County Firsts

☛ Austin County proudly refers to itself as a county of firsts. It is home to San Felipe, the state's first capital city and the location where the first book produced in Texas was published; the *Gazette*, the first newspaper, founded in 1829; the first postal system; the Texas Rangers, the state's first organized police force; the first Sunday school; the first flag and the official flag of independence; and the first English-speaking school, founded in 1829.

☛ The first organized church in Cherokee County was the Baptist Church, founded in 1844. It remains the predominant denomination of choice.

☛ Texas' first county fair was held at Fort Martin Scott in Gillespie County in 1881. The fair continued its annual festivities there until it was moved in 1889 to Fredericksburg.

Three Cheers for Longevity

Sweetwater was home to Faith, Hope and Charity Cardwell for most of their lives. The triplets, born on May 18, 1899, in Elm Mott, are thought to be the world's longest-lived triplets. Faith was the first of the trio to pass away in 1994 at the age of 95. Charity followed in 1995 and Hope in 1997. The triplets made it into the 2002 *Guinness Book of World Records*.

Holding Court

Donley County's claim to fame is in having the oldest courthouse in the Panhandle. Originally built for $28,500 in 1890, the century-old building recently underwent a restoration for a staggering $4.2 million.

IT'S ALL IN THE NAME

Here is a list of actual places to travel in Texas
(the number is the zip code):

Do you need to be cheered up? Why not visit:
      Comfort, 78013
      Friendship, 76530
      Happy, 79042
      Paradise, 76073
      Pep, 79353
      Rainbow, 76077
      Smiley, 78159
      Sweet Home, 77987
      Welcome, 78944

For sunlovers...
      Sun City, 78628
      Sundown, 79372
      Sunny Side, 77423
      Sunray, 79086
      Sunrise, 76661
      Sunset, 76270

Are you hungry?
      Bacon, 76301
      Noodle, 79536
      Oatmeal, 78605
      Pancakc, 76538
      Rice, 75155
      Salty, 76567
      Sugar Land, 77479
      Turkey, 79261

And you can top it off with:
> Sweetwater, 79556

Why travel to other states and cities? Texas has them all!
> Colorado City, 79512
> Denver City, 79323
> Detroit, 75436
> Memphis, 79245
> Miami, 79059
> Nevada, 75173
> New Boston, 75570
> Reno, 75462
> Santa Fe, 77517
> Tennessee Colony, 75861

Feel like traveling outside the country? Don't bother buying a plane ticket!
> Athens, 75751
> Canadian, 79014
> China, 77613
> Egypt, 77436
> London, 76854
> New London, 75682
> Palestine, 75801
> Paris, 75460
> Turkey, 79261

No need to travel to Washington, DC
> Whitehouse, 75791

We even have a city named after our planet!
> Earth, 79031

And there's a city named after our state!
> Texas City, 77590

Feeling tired?
> Energy, 76452

Are you cold?
> Blanket, 76432
> Winters, 79567

Do you like reading about history?
> Alamo, 78516
> Goliad, 77963
> Gun Barrel City, 75156
> Santa Anna, 76878

Need office supplies?
> Staples, 78670

Men are from Mars, women are from:
> Venus, 76084

You guessed it...it's on the state line...
> Texline, 79087

For the kids...
> Elmo, 75118
> Kermit, 79745
> Nemo, 76070
> Sylvester, 79560
> Tarzan, 79783
> Winnie, 77665

Other Texas towns that will make you smile:

Baby Head, 78643

Bee House, 76525

Best, 76932, and Veribest, 76886

Bigfoot, 78005

Bug tussle, 75449

Cactus, 79013

Cut and Shoot, 77303

Dime Box, 77853

Ding Dong, 76540

Frognot, 75424

Hogeye, 75423

Hoop And Holler, 75561

Jot 'Em Down, 75469

Kickapoo, 75763

Muleshoe, 79347

Notrees, 79759

Skeeterville, 79080

Telegraph, 76883

Telephone, 75488

Twitty, 79079

Uncertain, 75661

Whiteface, 79379

The anti-Al Gore city:

Kilgore, 75662

Don't forget...

Farewell, 79325

And, of course, there is a place in Texas that is...

Knott, Texas, 79748

TOP 10 REASONS TO LIVE IN TEXAS

10. Hello? It's Texas! Where else would you want to live?

9. It's illegal in Texas to put graffiti on someone else's cow. With 16 million of them, it's nice to know someone's worried about hide integrity.

8. Winter consists of snow flurries for one week—in Amarillo.

7. You don't measure distance in miles, you measure it in drive time.

6. The flag looks cool as a license plate and a t-shirt.

5. It's the only state where you can find both the biggest medical center and the biggest university—so if you've got an exotic disease, you can not only find someone who can pronounce it, you can also find someone who can fix it.

4. The official state snack is tortilla chips and salsa.

3. There are 1.2 roller coasters for every one million people.

2. Armadillos are just as likely to be decorative lamps and handbags as they are to be roadkill.

1. Y'all is recognized as the plural form of "you." Fixin' (as in "I'm fixin' to leave for the game") and sh**load (as in "I've got a sh**load of work to do today!") are also Texan.

ABOUT THE AUTHOR

Winter D. Prosapio

Winter Prosapio is a humor columnist, freelance writer and a media relations expert who has extensive experience working for Fortune 500 companies and nonprofit organizations. She is also a full-time mother, and care of her two children provides much of the fodder for "Crib Notes," her regular humor column that appears in the *New Braunfels Herald-Zeitung*, which was the first German newspaper in Texas, established in 1852. Winter has also written for the *Christian Science Monitor*, *Working Mother* magazine, *Family Tree* magazine and the *San Antonio Express News*.

ABOUT THE AUTHOR

Lisa Wojna

Lisa Wojna, author of several other nonfiction books, has worked in the community newspaper industry as a writer and journalist and has traveled all over Canada, from the windy prairies of Manitoba to northern British Columbia, and even to the wilds of Africa. Although writing and photography have been a central part of her life for as long as she can remember, it's the people behind every story that are her motivation and give her the most fulfillment.

ABOUT THE ILLUSTRATOR

Peter Tyler

Peter is a recent graduate of the Vancouver Film School visual art and design and classical animation programs. Although his ultimate passion is in filmmaking, he is also intent on developing his draftsmanship and storytelling, with the aim of using those skills in future filmic misadventures.

ABOUT THE ILLUSTRATOR

Roger Garcia

Roger Garcia immigrated to Canada from El Salvador at the age of seven. Because of the language barrier, he had to find a way to communicate with other kids. That's when he discovered the art of tracing. It wasn't long before he mastered this highly skilled technique, and by age 14, he was drawing weekly cartoons for the *Edmonton Examiner*. He taught himself to paint and sculpt, and then in high school and college, Roger skipped class to hide in the art room all day in order to further explore his talent. Currently, Roger's work can be seen in a local weekly newspaper and in places around Edmonton, Alberta.